Price Control Mechanism in Arthasastra
Ratan Lal Basu

Price Control Mechanism in Arthasastra

Price Control Mechanism in Arthasastra

Contents

Chapter-1 : Introduction

1.1 Preface

In the conventional academic circles, we trace the origin of accounting, banking, commodity production and all other laws and concepts of economics and commerce in Britain, especially, the British Industrial Revolution of the late 18th century.

There are innumerable well written books and articles on the economic thoughts of Adam Smith, Mercantilists, Physiocrats and various western economic schools. As regards ancient economic ideas we may refer to Greek ideas, even to the Old Testament. Unfortunately, very little effort has been given to explore the economic ideas inherent in ancient Indian literature. Western education has generated a feeling of disdain for ancient Indian culture and tradition among a large number of intellectuals. On the other hand, many express the view (without any substantiation) that we had everything of modern knowledge in ancient Indian writings. From this mess of biased views it is very difficult to filter out the essential aspects of ancient Indian achievements in different branches of knowledge.

Under these circumstances, one showing interest in ancient Indian economic ideas is likely to come up against insurmountable barriers. One class of intellectuals hold the view that it is a sheer fantasy to conceive of the existence of analytical economic ideas in ancient Sanskrit literature. Others opine that it is all divine and beyond the scope of scientific study. It is more dangerous to project (deliberately or out of ignorance) ideas discovered in modern era into the ancient times with the claim that they had been discovered in those days. Bias either way, out of either disdains or pseudo patriotism for the motherland, are equally troublesome as regards unraveling the truth inherent in ancient Indian writings. So one, studying ancient Indian economic ideas, is to painstakingly guard against both of these faux pas.

In spite of all these hazards, many scholars, particularly during the high-tide of nationalist movement in the first half of the 20th century, attempted to make an objective and unbiased evaluation of ancient Indian economic ideas implicitly or explicitly contained in ancient Indian writings, particularly, the Arthaśāstra of Chanakya, alias Kauṭilya(the straightforward and matter of fact approach of the book itself makes it most suitable, among ancient Indian literature, for a scientific study). The objective observation of M. A. Buch is worth noting in this context. He opines that economic ideas are but reflections of actual economic conditions of society. In ancient India, since the sixth century B. C., there had been considerable development of trade, commodity production and cash economy. So, economic ideas naturally developed in order to provide guidelines to traders, manufacturers and the rulers whose income depended on prosperity of the economy.

To quote him: "In the same way in economics we cannot expect any approach to Mill and Nicholson, Marshall and Taussig among the ancient writers of vartta. On the whole, the manner of presentation was concrete. The aim of vartta was severely practical; its business was to guide the trader, the agriculturist, the cattle-trainer, the artisan, the director of industries, the statesman, the teacher, the cultivator." (Buch, 1979, p. 15). We can, by no means, expect the economic ideas associated with modern industrial economics in ancient Indian writings as there is no evidence of the existence of modern factory industries and industrial capitalism in those days. Nor does it imply that the purpose of research into ancient Indian economic thought is to try any ancient model as such for the modern Indian economy. Nevertheless, study of ancient Indian economic ideas is likely to endow us with a deeper insight into our culture and tradition and the inherent national characteristics. It is all the more so because long foreign domination and indiscriminate experiments, after independence, with imported foreign models, have generated much confusion. In fact, we can hardly select a suitable model for development, nor can we investigate the real causes of failure of models so far tried, unless we have a clear idea about the characteristics of our nation which have been distorted beyond recognition by colonial rule and experiments with foreign models. As a reaction to all these distortions, a school holding diametrically opposite view, that revival of ancient ideas and methods is going to solve all our problems and we have nothing to learn from the modern western civilization, has emerged. Both the opposing camps have built up their views on sheer dogmas. So, an objective study is necessary. It is not a quest for the golden mean. May be ancient ideas are not at all relevant for modern India, may be they are sufficient to provide the complete guidelines for the course of our economic development, may be a 'golden mean' is the best choice. We, however, cannot come to any definite conclusion on the basis of preconceived rigid dogmas. Only an unbiased objective study can provide the right answer.

As regards the utility of the study of ancient Indian literature in connection with devising policies suitable to Indian tradition and objective conditions, Aiyanger observes, "——the historical interpretation of old systems of social thought, such as may result from a comparative study with their analogues, may help us to realize how social institutions have to be adjusted to the needs of the times, and how systems of thought have to be interpreted in connection with their peculiar purposes. The old Indian literature to which by analogy Cameral designation has been suggested may still be of value. Let us consider its skilful adaptation of means to ends, its logical deduction of rules of conduct from its socio-religious hypothesis, and its attempt to combine ethical, political and economic purposes in individual and social action. The attempt to view their teachings in their natural perspective and to interpret them in relation to our times as well as theirs might help in the dawn of the brighter day for which we all wait and hope." (Aiyanger, 1949, op. pp. 175-76)

According to Aiyanger, the following aspects of ancient Indian state policies, as delineated in Arthaśāstra, are likely to be relevant for the mixed economy of present day India:

i) In the Arthaśāstra state, freedom and regulations were intermixed. (p. 156)

ii) Large scale undertakings were taken over by the state management but scope was left for small enterprises to compete with state enterprises. (pp. 156-57)

iii) State factories did not displace private enterprises, nor penalize them (p. 157).

iv) Outside the spheres of state monopoly there was no attempt to compete with or restrain the private producer. (p. 157)

v) In the interest of the whole community, there were state regulations as regards interest, wages, profits and rent. But the state's position was that private liberty should be the rules except where it had to be restrained and regulated either in the interest of the common people or to maintain stability. (p. 157)

vi) Emphasis was laid on precision, simplification, detail and transparency as regards all state affairs, e.g.,

a) All state orders should be in writing.

b) Power and duties of different departments should be clearly demarcated.

c) Salaries of all public servants should be paid promptly.

d) Accurate data should be available as regards land surveys, fiscal collections, types of consumption etc. (p. 165)

Notwithstanding the difference in political system, the above six features of the Arthaśāstra state are not unsuitable for present day India. If properly adapted and implemented, they are likely to streamline the functioning of the various economic policies of the government today and remove many hurdles on the path of successful implementation of these policies.

There are, however, various obstacles on the path of unravelling the truth inherent in ancient Indian literature. Unlike the study of the west, it is not at all easy to dig out clear-cut and uncontroversial ideas from the vast body of ancient Indian literature. The Greeks were well known for historical writings. The tradition was carried on during the Roman and subsequent periods. Unfortunately, we do not have such coherent record of ancient Indian history. The otherwise rich Sanskrit literature of ancient India is overwhelmingly deficient in chronological history. To quote Kosambi:

"India has virtually no historical records worth the name......... In India there is only vague popular tradition, with very little documentation above the level of myth and legend. We cannot reconstruct anything like a complete list of kings. Sometimes whole dynasties have been forgotten. What little is left is so nebulous that virtually no dates can be determined for any Indian personality till the Muslim period ...... Certainly, no ancient Indian history is possible with the detailed accuracy of a history of Rome or Greece." (Kosambi, 1981, pp. 9-10)

Information regarding ancient Indian conditions are scattered in the Vedas, Purānas, the epics (Rāmāyana and Mahābhārata), the Dharmaśāstras, the Dharmasūtras, the Jātakas and Arthaśāstra of Kautilya (no other Arthaśāstra has yet been discovered). Excavations and inscriptions are other sources of information. Greek historical writers like Scylax, (c. 509 B. C.), Hecataeus, Herodotus, Ctesias, (survives only in abridged version by Photius), Nearchus, (survives in works of Strabo and Arrian), Onesicritus, Diogenes, Kleitarchus, and, especially, Megasthenes (fragments of his 'Indika' survives in the works of Strabo, Arrian, Diodorus and Plinius) provide valuable information regarding ancient Indian history along with its social, political and economic conditions. (Śāstri, K. A. Nilakanta (ed.) pp. 82-90). But it is very difficult to piece together the fragments of information obtained from diverse sources and construct a coherent economic history of ancient India.

In spite of these problems associated with the paucity of historical records, painstaking study and research are likely to bring out many valuable facts of ancient Indian economy. Max Müller rightly observed (quoted in Samaddar, 1922, pp. 4-5): "Depend upon it, there are enough of fields and pastures anew, for you to work .... you would be, not only unearthing the glories of your mother country, but you would be advancing towards higher points and nobler aims."

In the present study, we concentrate on a particular piece of ancient Indian literature, viz., Arthaśāstra of Kauṭilya. Many problems associated with the study of ancient Indian literature are likely to come up on the path of serious research on Arthaśāstra of Kauṭilya. But one advantage in this case is that, unlike much important ancient Indian literature, the entire Arthaśāstra is coherent, objective and analytical and is not shrouded in mystery, metaphors and myths. The matter-of-fact presentation, practical and realistic approach, simplicity of style and freedom from utopia make it most suitable for analytical study.

Discovery of the manuscript of Arthaśāstra of Kauṭilya by Shyamaśāstry and resurgence of Indian Nationalism stimulated the study of Arthaśāstra during the first half of the twentieth century, but, unfortunately, many of the works were marred by parochial views and wrong interpretation. To quote Aiyanger:

"The discovery and developments of Arthaśāstra studies in our generation have coincided with the resurgence of Indian Nationalism. While it has stimulated the study of the subject, it has also endangered the correct perception of its teachings, affiliations and methods. Incorrect notions gained ground and have become almost 'academic myths.' The attitude of Arthaśāstra to absolutism has been understood in a haze created by wrong interpretation and by the resurrection of legends, which grew round Chanaky. .... Its position in the orthodox canon, its relation to Dharmaśāstra, its attitude to the fundamental aims of life (as conceived in Ancient India), its 'secularism', its adaptability to environment and circumstances, its conception of law and the legislative power of the state and its ethics have been incorrectly grasped .... Much of the error may be traced to overlooking the study of the background of Indian life, which is common to both Arthaśāstra and Dharmaśāstra." (Aiyanger, 1949, Preface, pp. XII-XIII)

In this study, we take up a specific aspect of the economic policies prescribed in Arthaśāstra, viz. the price control mechanism. The choice springs from two basic reasons. First, very little light has been focused on this aspect in the existing literature on Arthaśāstra. Second, the price control mechanism, as prescribed in Arthaśāstra, appears to have some relevance for India today. The failure of price policy during the plan period in India is mainly due to the fact that it was framed in isolation without giving due regard to the legal and administrative set up necessary for its success. As a striking contrast, the price policy as prescribed in Arthaśāstra was inexorably associated with the legal and administrative mechanism. Can we emulate them in modern India to chalk out a meaningful price policy? What are the modifications necessary in view of the differences in the political systems of ancient India and modern India? Is the policy chalked out for a monarchic system at all relevant for a democratic set up? These are the pertinent questions to be investigated.

The legal and administrative set up in the age of Arthaśāstra was an integral part of price policy and without them price policy as prescribed in Arthaśāstra could not be properly implemented. So we ought to look into these measures, devised for proper implementation of our policy. But before that we should have some idea about the book itself on which our investigation is based.

1.2. Importance of Arthaśāstra in Economic Literature:

The subject matter of the present study is based on Arthaśāstra of Kauṭilya (the other well-known names of the author are Chanakya and Viṣṇugupta, who was the Prime Minister and Chief Adviser of Chandragupta Maurya, the founder of the Maurya dynasty. There are many legends (sometimes contradicting one another) about the life and education of Chanakya, the connotation of his pejorative nickname Kauṭilya (the plain meaning is crooked in nature), his relations with Chandragupta, his vengeance against Nanda dynasty, etc. but these legends and stories are not of much significance for our present study.

Discovery of the Manuscript

Mention of the magnum opus Arthaśāstra and partial quotes from it could be found in various available ancient Indian texts. References of this book were found in other available ancient Sanskrit literature, e.g. 'Nītisara' of Kāmandaka, 'Daśa Kumāra Charita' of Daṇḍin etc. (Shamaśāstry (ed.) 1967, Preface, pp. VII-VIII). But the manuscript of the original text was not available to the scholars till 1909. The existence of a manuscript of Kauṭilya's Arthaśāstra came to light in 1902 by Shamaśāstry, the then librarian of Oriental Manuscripts Library of Mysore, when it was handed over to the Library by a Brāhmaṇa scholar of Tanjore district.

Shamaśāstry produced a tentative English translation of the text in Indian Antiquary in 1905 and the following years. The full text was edited and published by Shamaśāstry in 1909 (Ibid. Introductory note by J. F. Fleet, p. V). Comparing this text with citations and references in other ancient works, scholars and experts on ancient Indian literature agreed that Shamaśāstry's edition was really the copy of the work composed by Kauṭilya (Majumdar, R.C. 1960, P. 140).

'though the existing text is, perhaps, not absolutely word for word that which was written by Kauṭilya.' (Shamaśāstry (ed.) 1967, op. cit. p. V).

It is apprehended that many sections of the original work have been lost and there might be some interpolations by authors belonging to later generations (Ibid. p. IX; also Śāstri, K. A. Nilakanta (ed.) 1967, p.200).

Nevertheless the available text is rich in economic and other ideas and a reliable source of research on Kauṭilya's Arthaśāstra.

After publication of Shamaśāstry's edition, interest in the study of ancient Indian literature got a fillip. The text was translated in many Indian and European languages. Mahamahopadhyay T. Gaṇapati Śāstri conducted a search for other manuscripts of Kauṭilya's work, and embodied his discoveries in a new edition of the classic during 1924-25 with a commentary of his own, in which he used an ancient Malayalam commentary, which must have embodied much traditional interpretations of Kauṭilya's work. About the same time, came the index verborum to Kauṭilya by Shamaśāstry, the fragments of the old commentaries on Arthaśāstra by Bhaṭṭasvamin, edited by K. P. Jayaswal and A. Banerji Śāstri in 1926, and by Madhava-Yajvan, the 'Nayachandrika', edited by J. Jolly and Paṇḍit Udayvira Śāstri in 1924 (Aiyangar, 1949, preface, pp. XI-XII).

Arthaśāstra, in modern sense, means the 'science of economics'. But in ancient Indian literature, the term referred to the 'science of material gain' (Kosambi, 1981, p. 142). Although, ancient Indian Arthaśāstras were mainly concerned with the science of statecraft, they embodied, in a wider sense, technology and all knowledge of practical arts over and above politics (K. A. Nilakanta Śāstri (ed.), 1967, p.192).

According to Aiyangar, "Arthaśāstra constituted a combined group of social studies, in which the unity of human nature was reflected in a unity of scientific treatment." (Aiyangar, 1949, p.131). In this context, the distinction between Arthaśāstra and other śāstras of India, viz. Sūtras, Dharmaśāstras and Nitiśāstras, is worth noting.

Sūtras were brief descriptions of Vedic sacrifices, rituals, social custom and laws written in prose style, easy to comprehend by common people. Sūtra literature developed in between c. 700 B.C. to 200 B. C. (Tripathi, 1981, pp.56-59). Dharmaśāstras, which developed in between the advent of the Christian era and 500 A.D. were written in śloka and contained traditional teachings on Hindu Civil and Criminal laws. Nitiśāstras were mainly concerned with ethical teachings. In contrast to these śāstras, Arthaśāstras were preoccupied with the science of statecraft. But political concepts in Arthaśāstras were inextricably associated with economic, social and other aspects of practical life. Kauṭilya mentions the names of several earlier Arthaśāstra authors, cites from their works and expresses his views regarding their opinions in different specific contexts.

Kauṭilya's Arthaśāstra was the last text in the Arthaśāstra tradition. From Kauṭilya's analysis of earlier Arthaśāstras, it appears that he had a thorough knowledge of them and in connection with various issues like the appointment of ministers, revenue collection, punishment for different offences, training of government officials, price fixation etc., he expressed his own views contradicting many of them after thoroughly consulting and scrutinizing the views of his predecessors on these issues. In fact, ideas embodied in Kauṭilya's Arthaśāstra are founded upon the vast resources of earlier Indian literature. But his pragmatic and secular views and coherent logic distinguishes him not only from the earlier Arthaśāstra compilers but also from the authors of other śāstras and philosophical treatises of ancient India.

Many modern scholars on ancient Indian literature are of opinion that the evolution of ideas that culminated in the great work of Kauṭilya was a reflection of the evolution of political, economic and social forces in ancient India. According to Kosambi, political thinking in ancient India kept pace with the evolution of political systems in the real world. The gradual development of political events ultimately culminated in the Maurya Monarchy, which used to control a vast geographical region extending from the northern end of the Indian subcontinent to Mysore in the South and Afghanistan in the west. Along with the evolution of the state, political theories also evolved by continuously adapting themselves to new political set ups in the real world and, in this process, culminated in the Arthaśāstra of Kauṭilya. Kosambi has furnished a mention-worthy explanation of this evolution from the standpoint of economic logic. According to him, rapid development of commodity production and extension of overland trade necessitated the emergence of a centralized monarchy with a strong administrative machinery so as to facilitate unhindered flow of goods across the entire Indian subcontinent. This economic factor was at the very root of the evolution of the political forces that led to the emergence of the vast Maurya Empire (Kosambi, 1981, pp.118-121). K. A. Nilakanta Śāstri attributes Kauṭilya's uniqueness among ancient Indian writers to a great extent to foreign influence. According to him, Kauṭilya was not only well versed with earlier Indian literature but also aware of foreign ideas pertaining to political economy, especially, administrative models prevalent in Egypt, Syria and Achaemenid Persia (K. A. Nilakanta Śāstri (ed.), 1967, p.3). He also opines that fiscal and bureaucratic arrangements in Arthaśāstra resembled that prevalent in Egypt and Syria contemporary to Kauṭilya (Ibid. p.174).

The uniqueness of Kauṭilya's Arthaśāstra is most strikingly revealed in the enhanced power of the king that Kauṭilya prescribed for. He held royal decree above sacred law (Dharma), private treaty, social usage, exalted reason (nyaya), and prescriptions of śāstras (Shamaśāstry (ed.), 1967, Book-II, Ch-I, pp.172-173). Thus, in contrast to the ancient Indian tradition of considering the king to be only the guardian of the law, not its maker, Kauṭilya made a bold departure to consider the king to be the law maker, and in case of any conflict, the king's edict is to prevail upon sacred law (Dharma), evidence (vyavahara) or history (charitra) (Ibid. p.172). According to Nilakanta Śāstri, Kauṭilya's radical departure from traditional practices was due to the influence of similar practices by contemporary Hellenic monarchies. But he asserts that Kauṭilya's treatise was not a mere copy of foreign ideas, but a harmonious assimilation of foreign ideas in accordance with the indigenous objective conditions (Nilakanta Śāstri (ed.), 1967, pp.174-175).

While studying Arthaśāstra, the question comes up in the readers' mind if it is the description of the actual political system of the Mauryan Era. It is difficult to come to a definite conclusion in this regard. From the style of the text, however, it appears that the approach is 'normative', i.e. what should be in an ideal prosperous and strong monarchic state rather than the photocopy of any existing political system. In this regard the views of P. C. Chunder are worth quoting:

"Kauṭilya's Arthaśāstra is not meant to be a photographic representation of an existing empire. Rather it furnishes a blueprint for a would-be conqueror (vijigīṣu). It teaches him how to be an emperor, the head of a circle of states (cakravartin)." (Chunder, 1995, p.27)

The treatise deals exhaustively with statecraft, economics, espionage, administration, war science, ecology and various other aspects pertaining to human living. The entire text is divided into fifteen books, each containing several chapters. Although there are occasional insertions of prose, the treatise is written mainly in ślokas (Sanskrit verse consisting of two lines).

Now let us have a brief glimpse of administrative, legal and other measures delineated in the text.

1.3. Political and Administrative Setup

Arthaśāstra of Kauṭilya puts forward price policy and many other economic policies. But these policy prescriptions were not isolated ones. They were, in fact, integral parts of the political, legal and administrative set up. In Arthaśāstra, economic policy measures are always accompanied by the necessary administrative and legal measures for proper implementation of these policies. So a glimpse of these measures is necessary to grasp the significance of the economic policies.

The political system to which Kauṭilya's Arthaśāstra refers is monarchy. A king in ancient India could not enjoy absolute power, nor could he become an autocrat because there were several checks and restrictions on him. He was to strictly adhere to the norms laid down in the śāstras, had to follow a tight routine and to endeavour to bring about prosperity and happiness to the people (Aiyangar, 1949, p.155).

Both Jayaswal (1967) and Altekar (1962) opine that the checks on the king were inherent in the political system.

But Kauṭilya made a radical departure from this age-old norm. He provided more discretionary power to the king. The king was no longer a puppet to enforce the laws embodied in the śāstras, but had the power to apply his own judgement while the necessities of time demanded a change in the existing canons of the śāstras (Arthaśāstra, Book – III, ch.1: 39-45).

This by no means gave the king power to be a self-seeker or to indulge in autocratic activities harming common people. The king could exercise his discretion to override existing practices only if it was necessary for the growth and maintenance of a strong and prosperous state and a centralized monarchy embracing a vast geographical region. Kauṭilya laid down in detail the methods to subjugate the independent corporations and tribal republics like Kāmbojas, Surāṣṭras, Lichchhivikas, Vṛjikas, Mallakas, Madrakas, Kukuras, Kurus, Pāñcālas etc., and to bring them under the rule of the monarch (Ibid. XI/1/4). This was necessary to consolidate the centralized monarchic rule and do away with the existence of all independent warrior groups and republics of Kṣatriya tribes so that unhindered trade from one end of the Indian subcontinent to the other was facilitated. An integral part of this monarchic rule was the administrative system characterized by the existence of a strong bureaucracy and an espionage network.

1.3.1. Bureaucracy

The administrative setup in Arthaśāstra was designed to facilitate the functioning of monarchic rule and was based on a strong bureaucratic system. The text prescribes in detail the specific functions of the Chamberlain, Collector-general, Accountant, and the

Superintendents of Treasury, Mines, Mint, Ocean-mines and host of other departments (Ibid. Book-II).

The function of each department is clearly demarcated in the text. Kauṭilya's bureaucratic system appears to be free from redtapism and other vices that make bureaucracy a serious hindrance to free functioning of the state machinery now a days. Measures to prevent breeding of such vices are inherent in the structure and methods of functioning of the bureaucracy as prescribed in Arthaśāstra. The bureaucracy in Arthaśāstra was also a strong deterrent to emergence of military rule, "even after usurpation of power by a successful General, and this is to be ensured by the power and permanence of fiscal laws and of the bureaucracy." (Aiyangar, 1949, pp.167-68). The dynamic and flexible bureaucratic system was an integral part of monarchic rule as envisaged in Arthaśāstra. It was essential for the proper functioning of the monarchic rule as envisaged in the text. This does not, however, imply that we cannot have such an efficient and coherent administrative mechanism in any political system other than monarchy, e.g. we emphasize that operation of such a bureaucracy is, in no way, going to violate the provisions in the democratic constitution of India today. On the contrary, it would make our democracy more meaningful and facilitate proper implementation of various economic policies.

1.3.2. Spy Network

The administrative system as delineated in Arthaśāstra was characterized by the existence of a strong network of spies and secret agents. The various professions under which the spies are to disguise themselves have been specifies in the text with detailed description of specific functions of each category of spies. Spies are to disguise as merchants, ascetics, householders, prisoners, students, prostitutes etc.

Kosambi and Vincent Smith blamed Kauṭilya's state as unethical because of the wide use of espionage mechanism (Kosambi, 1981, p. 143; Smith, 1967, p. 147). We should mention in this connection that much of the horrible impression about Kauṭilya's espionage network spring from the legends grown around the drama "Mudra Rākṣasa" of Visakhadatta.

The global political scenario has radically changed since the time when Vincent Smith wrote his book on Indian History. The post-Second World War period has been characterized by widespread espionage networks by the modern states too. Activities of the CIA & FBI (USA), KGB & OGPU (erstwhile USSR), ISI (Pakistan), R&AW & CBI (India), Mossad (Israel), MI-16 (UK), MSS (China), BND (Germany), FSB (Russia), DGSE and erstwhile SDECE (France) are not in essence much different from that of Kauṭilya's espionage network (Blackstock, 1964; Dallin, 1955; Furago, 1961; Gramont, 1962). The legends of "Mudra Rākṣasa" pale into insignificance if we compare them with the activities (verified facts, not legends) of the modern espionage agencies mentioned above.

Bharati Mukherjee justifies the vast espionage network of Kauṭilya as an alternative to the quick transport and communication facilities which were lacking in Kauṭilya's time (Mukherjee, Bharati, 1976, p. 42).

In any case, exhaustive network of spies is unethical in essence and in a true democratic system, it is not at all desirable. In fact, unlike in the days of Kauṭilya, this mechanism is not at all necessary now a days to properly implement price policy, or, for that matter, any policy of the government, notwithstanding the vast increase in population, number of commodities and complications in the operation of the economic system over the last two millennia. The efficiency, quickness and power of computers and the internet in handling these changed situations can by no means be disregarded.

1.3.3. Accounting

Perfect accounting is an inexorable ingredient of successful implementation of any policy or program. Here also Arthaśāstra prescriptions deserve praise. The detailed and accurate methods of accounting, as delineated in Arthaśāstra , reminds one of the accounting methods of a highly developed capitalist economy. Salaries of all public servants should be paid on time, all state orders should be in writing, power and duties of all the departments should be clearly defined, separate registers should be maintained for every item and accounts should be regularly entered in the prescribed registers (Arthaśāstra, Book-II, ch.7).

II/7/2: There he should cause to be entered in the record-books: the extent of the number, activity and total (income) of the departments; the amount of increase or decrease in the use of the (various) materials, expenses, excess, surcharge, mixing, place, wages and labourers in connection with factories; the price, the quality, the weight, the measure, the height, the depth and the container in connection with jewels, articles of high value, of low value and forest produce; laws, transactions, customs and fixed rules of regions, villages, castes, families and corporations; the receipt of favours, lands, use, exemptions, and food and wages by those who serve the king; the receipt of jewels and land (and), the receipt of special allowances and (payments for) remedial measures against sudden calamities, by the king and his queens and sons; and payments and receipts in connection with peace and war with allies and enemies.

In these days, all these could be accomplished by using computers.

The accounting and auditing network of Kauṭilya had to be facilitated by immaculate weighing and measuring systems, minute and accurate units of length, weight, time and space, maintenance of weighing balance, weighing stones and other implements of measurement (Ibid. Book-II, chs. 19, 20). Punctuality in preparing and presenting accounts (with some grace period, if justifiable) is to be strictly maintained (Ibid. Book-III, ch-7/26-41). Kauṭilya also insists on collection of accurate data and statistical information. To quote:

II/35/4: And in them, (he should record) so many are persons belonging to the four varṇas, so many are farmers, cowherds, traders, artisans, labourers and slaves, so many are two-footed and four-footed creatures, and so much money, labour, duty and fines arise from them.

II/35/5: And of males and females in the families, he should know the number of children and old persons, their work, customs and the amount of their income and expenditure.

Kauṭilya had a deep insight into basic human nature. He was always aware that human frailties may come on the path of implementing any policy, and he also realized that at times punishment is more effective than moral suasion to prevent crimes. Therefore, pertaining to implementation of accounting methods, he prescribed punitive measures depending on the degree of offence to prevent corruption, negligence and mismanagement (Ibid. Book-II, chs. 8, 9)2.

1.4. Significance of Price Control

Inflation, i.e. persistent rise in the price level, is a common feature of all market economies. So the government of a country is to adopt various price control measures which are divided into three major categories: i) Monetary Policy, ii) Fiscal Policy and iii) Direct Control.

Generally, most of the countries, now a days, lay stress on monetary and fiscal measures as inflation is mainly caused by monetary and fiscal causes. The third measure, viz. direct control, is resorted to only as a temporary device. In contrast to the modern economic systems, monetary and fiscal causes were not of much significance in ancient economies. The nature of the monetary systems in those days left little scope for rapid increase in money supply. Credit instruments and banking systems being undeveloped, bank money could hardly lead to instability. In those days, the government always endeavoured to maintain a surplus budget and budget deficit was looked upon as a serious weakness of the government. So, fiscal causes could hardly lead to problems in the price front. But the traders and artisans, if left alone, would always charge unduly high prices in order to earn higher profits and thereby generate instability and cause hardships to the common people. To prevent this, direct price control by the state was always necessary to avoid disorder and hardships of common people. So prices could not be left to be determined directly by market forces.

as regards the necessity of price control in India today, L. K. Jha, the Ex-Governor of the Reserve Bank of India, pointed out (Jha, 1968, pp. 478-80) that price in an LDC like India cannot be left to be determined by market forces, where, instead of free competition, monopolistic control prevails. Food prices are to be stabilized as they lead to all round price increase. Savings gap and foreign exchange deficit are two other causes requiring price control. In India, there is the need for building up a wide range of facilities where commercial considerations of maximum direct return on investment do not or cannot always apply. Direct price control becomes necessary for the following reasons:

i) To protect the interests of the vulnerable sections of the population.

ii) To guide investment to desired channels.

iii) To prevent hoarders from increasing prices by taking advantage of shortages.

All these have become necessary because of certain specific circumstances and they are not inherent in the democratic system in India itself. But in Arthaśāstra , the price policy appears to be an integral part of a centralized administration where the state aimed at having control over all aspects of life. This, however, does not mean that the state wanted to make undue interference with economic and social activities. Control was resorted only to ensure that unrestricted freedom does not lead to disharmony and pursuits of self-interest by one class of people does not cause disadvantages and sufferings to other classes. Kauṭilya had deep insight into the nature of different classes of people. So he knew well that the merchant class, whose sole motive was to earn profit, would adopt unfair means to earn excessive profit unless controlled by the state. Activities of the traders which were likely to cause harm to the common people were:

i) Use of false weights, ii) Smuggling, iii) Profiteering, iv) Enhancement of profit by cornering commodities, and v) Adulteration.

Kauṭilya devised various punitive measures to prevent these mischiefs. (Arthaśāstra , book-II, ch-21, book-iv, ch-2)

Thus we see that, in spite of the differences in political systems, the basic objectives of price policy of Arthaśāstra did not differ, in essence, from the price policy in India during the plan period. But the following features of price policy of Arthaśāstra distinguish it from that of India at present.

i) No unnecessary control: centralization and state control were to be exercised only when it was necessary and the state should refrain from unnecessary controls (Book-II, ch-21).

ii) Commodities were to be sold only at specific market places (Ibid).

iii) Commodities were to be sold only after they are precisely weighed, measured, numbered and marked by government seal (Ibid).

iv) Commodities shall never be sold where they are grown or manufactured (book-II, ch-22).

v) The price, whatever it is, should be announced by the seller. The merchandise being placed near the flag of the toll-house, the merchants shall declare its quantity and price (book-II, ch-21).

vi) Price increase by haggling was discouraged. When the purchasers happens to bid for it, the enhanced amount of the price together with the toll on the merchandise shall be paid into the king's treasury (book-II, ch-21).

vii) Short term and long term aspects: Kauṭilya could recognize the forces (of demand and supply) that play the crucial role in determination of price. According to Arthaśāstra , prices are to be fixed by the state at specific levels only as a short term measure so that temporary fluctuations of demand and supply do not generate instability and cause hardships to common people, that the traders could not take undue advantage of the situation of temporary scarcity to enhance price in order to earn exorbitant profit and that temporary over-supply does not force the traders to incur losses. If, however, discrepancy between demand and supply persists over a long period, prices are to be readjusted in conformity with changes in demand and supply. But these adjustments are to be undertaken strictly by the state without any freedom for the private traders and artisans to readjust prices on their own.

viii) Buffer stock:

In Arthaśāstra much emphasis is laid on the maintenance of a buffer stocks of all commodities and replenishing them regularly so as to meet accidental shortages and thereby, to ensure smooth implementation of the price policy without any hardship of the common people in years of scarcity. .

II/15/22: From these he should set apart one half for times of distress for the country people, (and) use the

(other) half for times of distress for the country people, (and) use the (other) half.

II/15/23: And he should replace old (stock) with new.

The above mentioned features were essential for successful implementation of price policy of Arthaśāstra . They were devised with a monarchic rule in mind. But a deeper insight would reveal that they are not at all antagonistic to a democratic system, or, for that matter, any non-monarchic political set up. So, if these features turn out to be suitable for converting our, 'ill-administered' price policy into a 'well-administered' one, we may emulate them for meaningful implementation of the price policy of India today.

1.5. Survey of Existing Literature

Since the publication of Shamasastry's edited text and translation of Arthaśāstra , a large number of books and articles on Arthaśāstra and its author have been published. The subject matter of these works may be divided into the following major categories:

i) On the author and the period of Arthaśāstra .

ii) On the socio-political system delineated in Arthaśāstra and in the age of Arthaśāstra .

iii) On the economic system embodied in and in the age of Arthaśāstra .

1.5.1. On the Author and the Period of Arthaśāstra

As regards the first category, contributions of Shamasastry, Ganapati Sastri, Nilakanta Sastri, N. N. Law, V. A. Smith, Jolly, Meyer, Winternitz, P. C. Chunder, etc. are worth mentioning. There was a debate as regards the period of the text, identity of its author, authenticity of the author etc., without any definite conclusion. The polemic, however, is not of much significance for the present research work, as our study is based on the manuscript discovered by Shamasastry in 1902. So the identity of the author, the exact period of compilation of the text and the question of conformity of the text with some real politico-economic system are irrelevant in the context of our study. To quote Nilakanta Sastri (1967, p. 178):

"the Arthaśāstra , though to a large extent based on contemporary practice, is still a sastra, a normative plan rather than a description of existing conditions."

According to R. C. Majumdar (1960, p. 14):

"The newly discovered text fully sustains the reputation of the work, and its contents agree fairly well with the view that was formed about its scope and nature from the numerous references to and quotations from it in subsequent literature ... whatever view we might take, it would be convenient and in accordance with general usage to designate it as Kauṭilya Arthaśāstra , or simply Arthaśāstra without any qualification."

1.5.2. On the Socio-Political System

The second category of works deals with various aspects of political, administrative and legal systems prescribed in Arthaśāstra and prevalent in the period of Arthaśāstra . Authors like A. S. Altekar,

N. C. Banerjee, D. R. Bhandarkar, U. N. Ghosal, K. P. Jayaswal, P. V. Kane, R. K. Mookerji, B. Mukherjee, K. M. Panikkar, H. Roychowdhury, Nilakanta Sastri, Vincent Smith, etc. describe a political system which had evolved since the Vedic period to assume the form of monarchy of the Mauryan period. Along with the political system, political thought also evolved to culminate in Arthaśāstra of Kauṭilya. Nilakanta Sastri (1967) opines that Kauṭilya's political thought is a synthesis of Indian tradition and foreign ideas, especially, that from 'Achaemenid' Persia. Most of the above mentioned authors agree that the king in India could not become an autocrat because there were several checks inherent in the political system.

According to Altekar (1962, p. 57), Indian political thought was based on the Vedantic doctrine of 'karma' (work culture). Nilakanta Sastri (1967, p. 174) opines that Kauṭilya made a departure from the earlier sastras by putting the king above the sastras. According to Altekar, from the 4th century B. C. influence of theology on the state began to decline, and politics developed into a special science. There emerged a principle of statecraft that was to 'promote piety and religiousness by extending equal patronage to all sects and religions and to enforce customary laws approved by the social conscience.' (Altekar, 1962, p. 55)

Thus emerged a strong state embracing almost the whole of India and promoting unity among diversity. The theoretical counterpart of this sociopolitical development was Kauṭilya's Arthaśāstra . Kosambi (1981, pp. 120-132) opines that centralized monarchy of Magadha emerged in course of time as it was necessitated by continuous development of trade and commodity production.

Authors like Altekar, U. N. Ghosal, M. H. Gopal, B. C. Sen, R. Tripathi, D. D. Kosambi, etc. pointed out the existence of a strong bureaucratic machinery which was necessary for perfect functioning of the monarchic rule covering a vast geographical area. They emphasize that the strength and efficiency of the administrative machinery was based on perfect auditing and accounting and strictly regulated weights and measures. Aiyangar opines that the strong bureaucracy prevented the emergence of any military dictatorship. Authors like Jayaswal, V. D. Mahajan, R. C. Majumdar, R. K. Mookerji, H. Roychowdhury, etc. throw light on the local self- governments and decentralized administration. The local bodies including the village assemblies used to enjoy much power and autonomy. According to R. C. Majumdar, Panikkar and Mahajan, urban administration under municipal bodies was well organized and extremely efficient.

V. A. Smith, Keith, Kosambi, Bharati Mukherjee, etc. deal with the exhaustive and powerful espionage network. Kosambi and V. A. Smith consider the Kauṭilyan state unethical because of the wide use of espionage mechanism. In this regard Keith opines, "It would indeed be melancholy if this were the best that India could show...." (quoted in Kosambi, 1981, p. 141). Bharati Mukherjee (1976, p. 42), however, justifies the vast espionage network of Kauṭilya as an alternative to the quick transport and communications facilities which were lacking in Kauṭilya's time.

Altekar, B. C. Sen and Bharati Mukherjee deal in detail, with the welfare activities of the state in Arthaśāstra and opine that the state, Kauṭilya opted for, was a welfare state.

1.5.3. On the Economic System

The third category of authors deal with various aspects of the economic system in the Arthaśāstra state.

Authors like B. C. Sen, R. K. Mookerji and D. D. Kosambi give a detail description of the state sector. There was a large state sector and state ownership of mines, fisheries, transport and a significant portion of agriculture, industry and trade.

According to Kosambi, the Mauryan period and the contents of Arthaśāstra of Kauṭilya give evidence of highly developed commodity production and widespread commercialization of the economy. But the rural economy was hardly affected by this commercialization. A.

N. Bose, M. A. Buch, S. K. Das and R. K Mookerji corroborate this view regarding the dichotomy between the rural and the urban sectors. Changes over time left very little impression on the traditional rural sector. Kauṭilya, too, opted for a peaceful rural economy, undisturbed by the din and bustle of urban life.

According to R. K. Mookerji, punch-marked coins of silver and other metals became the chief currency at the Maurya period. But barter and use of 'cowrie shells' were still in use in certain localities. (Mookerji, 1980, pp. 607-608)

Kosambi, Mookerji, Panikkar and Nilakanta Sastri give an account of the remarkable development of internal and foreign trade. There were long trade routes extending from one end of the country to the other. Nilakanta Sastri (1967) mentions of foreign trade with Greek cities, West Asia and Egypt. Samaddar (1922) mentions seventeen provinces and countries with which India had foreign trade. [9] A. N. Bose (1945) mentions of overseas trade with Mesopotamia, Egypt, Arabia, Zambia, African Coast, Mediterranean Zone and Rome.

M. A. Buch (1979) discusses in detail the existence of a large number of handicrafts industries that had acquired remarkable skill at the time of Kauṭilya. A. N. Bose (1945) gives an account of the existence of division of labour. Panikkar (1966) gives an account of the power and status of trade and craft guilds. A. N. Bose opines that along with the development of trade and commerce there was considerable advancement of credit instruments and banking.

Authors like U. N. Ghosal, M. H. Gopal, R. K. Mookerji, H. C. Roychowdhury, N. Sastri etc. deal in detail, with public finance and fiscal policy as delineated in Arthaśāstra . The major sources of revenue of the state were income from state sector production and commercial activities and various indirect taxes on goods and services. Tributes, fines and licence fees were also parts of state revenue. State expenditure were incurred for defence, internal administration, maintenance of the royal family and various religious and social welfare activities of the state. As regards fiscal policy, special emphasis was laid on maintenance of a surplus budget.

Mookerji and B. C. Sen mention the existence of strict state regulation of artisans (who were organized in strong guilds) to protect the interests of the consumers and common people.

Determination and Control of Prices of Goods and Services and Factors of Production

Altekar (1949, p. 327) gives a brief account of the price policy in Arthaśāstra . According to him the superintendent of commerce used to control retail and wholesale prices of commodities and tried to ensure their steady supply through its market superintendents.

B. C. Sen (1967) gives a more elaborate account of price policy. Prices of final goods, interest rates, rents and profits are to be fixed by the superintendent of commerce. Wages are to be determined by contract between the clients and the artisans. But both the parties should strictly adhere to the terms and conditions of contract.

Goods cannot be sold at the place of production (field or factory) but should be transported to the specified market where the seller should declare the quantity, quality and prices of his goods. After proper examination, the market officials should get them registered in official books. Prices were fixed on the basis of 'cost plus reasonable profit' principle. Bargaining and bidding were prohibited. False statements regarding cost, etc., smuggling, adulteration, speculation, cornering of commodities and other malpractices were subject to severe punishment.

Now, the question arises: if the price policy delineated in Arthaśāstra could be implemented in reality; how the prices of final goods and factors would be determined in conformity with the Arthaśāstra principles; how the prices of different goods and services, available in those days, were interrelated; how the state would adjust different inter-related prices if prices of some commodities are readjusted on the basis of supply-demand situation. These are pertinent questions associated with the price policy in Arthaśāstra and inquiry into these aspects would reveal whether price policy statements in Arthaśāstra were mere statements or they had some realistic significance. None of the authors mentioned above, have, however, gone into these vital questions pertaining to the price policy in Arthaśāstra . So here is an important research gap relevant to Kauṭilya's Arthaśāstra and the present study is geared to venture into these hitherto overlooked aspects of Arthaśāstra .

1.6.1. Major Research Question

Form the survey of the existing works in the field, it is evident that there is a major research gap in the field. The price policy and price control mechanism in Arthaśāstra has not yet been dealt with in detail by any author or researcher on Arthaśāstra . So, the purpose of the present research work is to explore this un-trodden field. Perfect functioning of the Arthaśāstra economy depends on the financial soundness of the government, which again depends a good deal on the revenue collected from commodity taxes (ad valorem). So uncertainty and irregularity about prices of commodities would lead to uncertainty in the entire economic system as delineated in Arthaśāstra . The text itself states briefly that the government's price policy would result in stability and certainty in the price front. The question arises whether this was possible and if so, how the mechanism is likely to work. If it comes out that perfect implementation of price policy is not feasible, then the entire Arthaśāstra mechanism becomes questionable for reasons mentioned above. Thus it is a vital question to test if there was a realistic price control mechanism in Arthaśāstra set up and if so, what was the probable interrelations through which it worked. This study takes up this vital question which has not yet been explored by existing literature on Arthaśāstra.

Chapter-2: Economic System Prevalent in the Age of Arthaśāstra

2.1. Introduction

A close study of Arthaśāstra brings to the fore the picture of an integrated and well-ordered economic system of which price control mechanism was an integral part. An analysis of Arthaśāstra and various works on the text and the relevant historical epoch reveal the existence of a dualistic system with an urban sector characterized by commodity production and a traditional rural sector. Most of the primary commodities (as listed in the appendix to this chapter) were produced in the traditional sector. Because of the simple features of the rural economy and simple production mechanism, price determination of the primary commodities produced in this sector does not call for any complicated mechanism. On the other hand, determination of prices of commodities processed and traded in the urban sector calls for a sophisticated device. So, our mathematical model for price determination would be confined to the urban sector alone. Development of trade and transport network in those days facilitated the implementation of a uniform price policy for the entire country. So we should have a glimpse of the trading and transportation mechanism prevalent in the age of Arthaśāstra . At first sight, it appears that unlike in the modern economies, monetary and credit aspects did not have any appreciable impact on the price front. This matter is to be closely scrutinized. Fiscal policies in those days attempted to maintain a surplus budget. Thus fiscal aspect had little impact on prices. Revenue collection of the government depended a good deal on indirect taxes which used to influence prices at various stages. So an overall idea of revenue collection of the government, particularly, taxation mechanism, is necessary for price determination in the Arthaśāstra state. Before going into these matters, let us first have a glimpse of the dual aspect of the Arthaśāstra economy.

2.2. Dual Economy

The Arthaśāstra economy may be split up into two distinct sectors: the traditional rural sector and the organized urban sector. The tiny urban sector had to depend on the vast rural sector for food and other primary consumption goods and raw materials to be processed in the urban sector. On the other hand, dependence of the rural sector on the urban sector was minimal. The simple rural life in those days did not call for much consumption goods from the urban sector. Moreover, as would be seen below, there were strict prohibitions on inflow of amenities from the urban sector to the rural sector. It appears that the simple implements required for primary sector production (ropes, baskets, etc.) could be produced within the primary sector itself. Instruments like plough-heads, various implements for digging earth and mines, sickles, knives, metallic pots, etc. had to be bought from the urban sector. But considering the life span of these instruments, contributions, of these instruments and devices to the cost of production of primary products, may be considered to be negligible. All these would be clear if we have a closer view of the rural economy.

2.2.1. Rural Economy

From the description of Arthaśāstra (Book-II, ch-1), it appears that the majority of the population of the Arthaśāstra state lived in villages which were kept free from the influence of the cash economy of the urban sector (Book-II, ch-1). In stark contrast to the urban commercialized sector, the rural sector was characterized by primitive features of a typical traditional society. According to R. C. Majumdar (1960, p. 150), most of the royal dues and taxes from villages were paid in kind – some villages supplied soldiers, some grains, some raw materials, some cattle, some dairy products, etc. R. K. Mookerji (in Majumdar (ed), 1980, p. 607) observes that in the rural sector, the old system of barter was still in existence. The cultivators had to work on their fields like 'robots' in complete isolation from the din and bustle of city life. Agriculture was held in such a high esteem in those days that even the invading soldiers did not disturb agricultural pursuits of the country invaded. To quote Kosambi:

"Greek observers of the fourth century noted with amazement that these peasants (georgoi) would continue to plough their fields in stolid indifference to armies fighting pitched battle within sight. No wonder, because the laws of war gave the totally disarmed Śūdra farmer personal immunity, and whoever won could make no difference to his way of life" (Kosambi, 1981, p. 151). Elsewhere (Ibid. p. 157), Kosambi depicts a vivid picture of the rural economy: "Only it must be remembered that by far the greater number of people lived in deaf sītā villages, where every precaution was taken to keep them hard at work on the soil. The prostitute, wine shop and gambling house were amenities for the cities and towns, not for the country side in general. When we say that the Magadhan state and its society reduced everything to its money equivalent, the statement applies primarily to urban life, to caravan trader, and the state official; not to lowly peasant deported for settlement on crown land."

A. N. Bose (1945, vol. II, p. 183) described similar contrast between rural and urban sectors of ancient India: "The essential difference was in the economic structures of towns and villages. The villages were the productive units of the country given to tillage and small handicrafts. The towns were centres for distribution and exchange, of big business and industrial combines where, besides its own wealth, the wealth of the country accumulated and attracted in its turn learning and culture as well as luxuries and parasite professions ...... The jealous attempt to guard agriculture against the corrupting diversions of the town shows clearly that there was a deep-seated difference and loss of contact between town life and country life."

All agricultural and primary commodities and presumably some handicraft products were to be brought to the towns from the rural sector by traders so as to meet food and other consumption requirements of urban dwellers and raw material requirements of urban crafts. The prices of these commodities at urban centres contained collection cost (which we would assume to be given, as our interrelated price determination model is meant for the urban sector alone), transport cost and toll charges.

Now let us look into the features of the urban sector

2.2.2. Urban Economy

It is a matter of surprise that more than two thousand years before the emergence of modern capitalism, the urban sector in India, based on handicraft industries alone, revealed many features of modern market economies. The vivid description of the cash economy in Arthaśāstra (Book-II, chs-12-15), the detailed operations of preparation of flour from wheat in husking mills, edible oils from oil seeds, yarn from cotton, blankets from wool, furniture from timber, smelting of various grades of ores, etc. drew the attention of authors like Kosambi, who comments that this unique feature of commodity production and cash economy of the urban sector distinguished the Arthaśāstra economy from any other ancient economy in India or elsewhere (Kosambi, 1981, p. 152). He observes: "We might be reading a factory production manual rather than a book on statecraft."

Another notable feature of the cash economy delineated in Arthaśāstra was that production, in both the private and the state sectors, was meant for sale and not for self-consumption. The goods produced in the state sector were sold to the traders and to other state departments in exchange for cash and with full account (Book-III). Every state servant was paid in cash (Book-v ch-3). Even compulsory 'vishti' labourers were paid in cash (Book-v, ch-3). The cash appraisal of everything was also reflected in the table of fines (Shamasastry, 1967, pp. 478-83). Thus we see that cash economy penetrated every corner of urban life in the Arthaśāstra state. This distinguished the Arthaśāstra state from all forms of feudal system.

The commercial urban sector was accompanied by an industrial sector comprising a large number of highly efficient crafts, many of which originated as early as the Vedic period. M. A. Buch (1979, vol-I, pp. 116-197) cites the existence of the following crafts during this period: textiles (cotton, silk, woolen), perfumes, glassworks and mirrors, umbrellas, leatherworks and shoes, woodworks, stone-works, ivory-works, ornaments, mining and metallurgy (gold, silver, iron, tin, lead etc.). The artisans, in each branch of craft, had acquired remarkable skill because of conducive socio-economic and political set up (Ibid. pp. 202-236).

Most of the products of these crafts have been mentioned in Arthaśāstra (a complete list given in the Appendices to this chapter). According to Arthaśāstra principles, no goods could be sold at the place of origin (Book-II, ch-22). So, they are to be carried to the appointed market place and sold to the traders who would distribute them throughout the country according to demand. At every sales point, tolls and other charges are to be paid to the relevant government officials. Wide distribution of commodities was possible because of developed transportation and trading system. We are going to have a glimpse of these matters in the next section. But before that, a few observations about the nature of technology of these crafts are necessary. This is done in the sub-section below.

2.2.3. Technology

By the time of Arthaśāstra the methods of production in all branches of craft had become highly sophisticated, leaving no scope for change inspired by individual talent and desire for variety. In fact, historically achieved tradition and stereotyped methods of production had to be pursued by each artisan. All individual talent and desire for change had to be sacrifices at the altar of historically achieved impersonal rules (Buch, 1979, vol-I, pp. 194-96). Meticulous specifications of the production of different commodities in Arthaśāstra also corroborate this view.

So, we may consider technology and input specifications of production of each commodity to be given. Regional variations in in specifications of inputs is not likely to impose any problem as, in Arthaśāstra , products are mentioned along with the names of the places of production and so the same commodity produced at different localities may be considered as separate commodities, e.g. cotton fabrics produced at Kalinga and Vanga are called Kalingaka and Vangaka and treated as different commodities. We would indicate given technology by the following notation:

For any given I and j,

aij, the amount of the ith input needed to produce one unit of the jth commodity, is assumed to be constant for all levels of output, i.e. we assume constant returns to scale. Input substitution is ruled out as it becomes evident from the study of the guild system that the powerful guilds were likely to take care that the specified inputs for a product are not substituted by inferior varieties and the traditionally given sacrosanct input specifications are not violated by individual artisans.

2.3. Trade, Commerce and Transport

Arthaśāstra itself and writings of foreign authors of this period (Megasthenes and others) reveal the existence of highly developed transport and communication facilities that interconnected different parts of the country facilitating free flow of goods and services throughout the country. Along with internal trade, foreign trade also flourished during this period. Development of trade and transport system facilitated the implementation of a uniform price policy by the government.

2.3.1. Internal Trade

At the time of compilation of Arthaśāstra , there was considerable development of internal trade. A large community of traders emerged during this period. They used to carry goods from one end of the country to the other. This was facilitated by development of transportation system by state initiative. The state always encouraged trade and free flow of goods and services throughout the entire country, from rural to urban areas and among various urban centres. We have already discussed in Chapter-I that necessity of countrywide trade led to the emergence of a centralized monarchy embracing a vast geographical region. It appears from the study of Arthaśāstra that various crafts were located at various parts of the country. This becomes clear from the attachment of names of localities to different commodities in Arthaśāstra . It is quite natural that by tradition, suitable climatic conditions and availability of inputs, production of a specific commodity was localized at a specific region. But trade ensured the flow of each commodity to wherever it was demanded, either as a consumer good or as an input. A. N. Bose (1945, vol-II, p. 280) opines in this connection: "The self-sufficiency and isolation of gamas and janapadas were broken by active trade and long highways of commerce intersecting between them stimulated by localization of industries." Urban centres located at various parts of the country were separated from one another by villages. Arthaśāstra (Boo-II, ch-1) specifies the construction of fortified urban centres – a *sthānīya* among 800 villages, a *droṇemukha* among 400 villages, a *khārvāṭika* among 200 villages and a *saṅgrahana* among 10 villages. The urban centres were to be connected by suitable roads. Different regions of the country were at places isolated by hilly and desert tracts and deep forests. The government had to construct roads and take adequate measures (safeguards against probable hazards) to facilitate trade among the distant and isolated regions of the country.

In those days, overland trade routes linked the middle Ganges valley with

a) The upper Godavari valley and the South-Western Coast,

b) The lower Ganges valley and the Eastern Coast,

c) The Sindhu and the Indus delta,

d) The Indus valley and the Gāndhara which was again roadlinked with the South-Western Coast (A. N. Bose, 1945, vol-II, p. 286).

Nilakanta Śāstri (ed, 1967, p. 269) mentions four major internal trade routes, viz. East to West, North to South-West, North to South-East and North-West routes linking the major cities and trading centres like Champa, Benares, Pataliputra, Nalanda, etc. and the great highway of Central and Western Asia. A fair part of inland trade was carried along the water routes – the Ganges, Jamuna, Godavari and many small rivers and their tributaries. Large boats were available on hire for this purpose (A. N. Bose, 1945, vol-II, p. 292). Trade along long distant land routes were carried on by caravans. Kosambi (1981, pp. 125-26) gives a vivid description of caravan trade.

Journey of the trading caravans through dense forest, deserts and other difficult terrains was fraught with various hazards. Rivers without bridges had to be crossed by ferries. The merchants had to hire forest guards to cross the forests and land pilots to cross the deserts at night (Arthaśāstra , Boo-II, chs-4, 11, 12; Book-VII, ch-12; N. Sastri, ed, 1967, p. 270). Notwithstanding state help and encouragement, countrywide flourishing trade, under the above mentioned hazardous conditions, could not have been possible without the existence of a dynamic and adventurous trading class. In fact, this trading class became the dominant economic force to shape the political destiny of the country in those days. N. Sastri (ed, 1967, pp. 271-72) and Kosambi (1981, pp. 120-127) have described in detail how the rise of the Nanda dynasty and later on, Maurya dynasty paved the way for political unification of India (by subjugating the tribal republics)1, under a centralized monarchy which facilitated countrywide unhindered trade. According to Kosambi, evolution of trade had its political counterpart in the centralized monarchic rule.

State help provided to encourage trade were:

i) Construction of roads and highways (Book-II, ch-4)

ii) Manufacture of trading vehicles, boats etc. in the state sector (Book-II, chs- 18, 33)

iii) Construction of market towns (Book-II, ch-1)

iv) Provision of security to traders and protection against wild animals, corrupt government officials, theft and robberies (Book-II, ch-2, Book-IV, chs- 10, 12)

v) Management of waterways, provision of ferry services by the state, etc. (Book-II, ch-18)

vi) Various state regulations to facilitate orderly trade, e.g. price-control; restriction on haggling and bargaining; measures against adulteration, smuggling and other malpractices by artisans and traders; compulsion to sell goods at specified market places only, etc.

development of inland trade and commerce, under the patronage of the state, facilitated the implementation of a uniform price policy.

2.3.2. Foreign Trade

Along with inland trade foreign trade was also encouraged and facilitated by an efficient administrative mechanism. Arthaśāstra mentions various goods of foreign origin. In our Price Control Model, however, we do not give any separate treatment to goods of foreign origin. Moreover, information in this regard is so insignificant (both in the text itself and in the writings about the relevant time) that an open-economy model of price determination is not possible. It may be presumed that internal production in those days was not appreciably influenced by and dependent on foreign trade. Nonetheless, we may have a cursory glance at the condition of foreign trade in those days. 2

According to the Greek writers, India's foreign trade was carried on by partly land route and partly sea route McCrindle, 1877)3. According to A. N. Bose (1945, vol-II, pp. 279-299), overseas trade of India developed with African Coast, Mediterranean Zone, Arabia, Mesopotamia, Egypt, Zambia and Rome. There were arrangements of toll concessions to foreign traders (Book-II, ch-16).

2.3.3. Organization of Trade and Industry

The Arthaśāstra state was characterized by the existence of strong and well organized guilds which acted like modern monopolies and cartels and were likely to charge exorbitant prices at the cost of the customers unless regulated by the state. Kauṭilya was well aware of the monopoly power, profit motive and anti-people attitude of the artisans and traders organized in guilds. He opines: "Thus let the king prevent these thieves such as merchants, craftsmen .... and others, although they are not called thieves in spite of oppressing the country" (Book-IV, ch-1, Chunder, 1995, p. 248). That this apprehension of Kauṭilya was not unfounded would be clear if we look at the power of the trade and craft guilds in those days. Trade and industry, during the period of Arthaśāstra, was organized under strong guilds which had evolved since the Vedic times. Almost every important craft or occupation in a locality used to form a guild. Persons belonging to each craft used to acquire their profession by heredity, used to settle in a well-defined locality and were organized under a 'Jettaka' or 'Pamukha'. The guilds possessed both executive and judicial power and were entitles to arbitrate between its members through executive officers. Some of the guilds used to maintain regular army ready to serve the king whenever called upon. Sometimes a number of guilds got united under a federation presided over by a "Bhāṇḍagārika". Merchants used to form guilds under chiefs called 'Setthis'. Travelling traders used to form guilds under 'Satthavahas' (Mookerji in Majumdar, ed, 1980, pp. 601-602). Panikkar (1966, p. 36) opines that guilds used to enjoy great economic and political power.

Kauṭilya devised special measures to force these strong guilds to conform to the price policy of the government. Kauṭilya prescribed elaborate fines and other forms of punishment for exorbitant prices and fees, false weights, adulteration and similar mischiefs committed by profit mongering artisans and traders belonging to monopolistic guilds (Book-IV, chs- 1 and 2).

2.4. Monetary Policy, Currency and Coinage

Now a days, monetary policy plays an important role in regulation of prices in almost all the modern economies. Deficit financing, too much supply of currency notes, expansion of bank credit, etc. are the major causes of inflation now a days. In fact, the inflationary process in India since the Second Five Year Plan was initiated mainly by deficit financing. So, tight-money policy is considered as an important device to control inflation.

But in the days of Arthaśāstra, money supply could hardly create any pressure on the price level. Paper currency was unknown in those days. Currency circulated used to consist of metallic coins (of gold, silver, copper and alloys) which were scarce in supply. Monetary policy of the government was geared to meet the circulatory requirements of the economy and evidences reveal that money supply was at times scarce vis-à-vis demand. According to Mookerji (in Majumdar, ed, 1980, pp. 607-08), in rural segment and distant localities , barter and use of 'Cowrie Shells' as medium of exchange were still in vogue. Banking system was at a rudimentary stage and bank credit had insignificant role in the economic system.

Thus it appears that unlike the modern states, the Arthaśāstra state did not require monetary measures to regulate prices. Now let us look into the salient features of the money and credit system of the Arthaśāstra state.

2.4.1. Currency and Coinage

Along with the development of trade and commodity production since the Vedic times, the coinage system also went through a process of development and , in conformity with the levels of advancement of trade and commodity production, achieved a high level of development during the period of Arthaśāstra.

At the earliest stage, pieces of metals of various specified weights and shapes without any official stamp were used as coins, e.g. the Vedic gold coins like 'Nishka', 'Satamana', and 'Suvarna'. At the next stage, metal pieces of particular shapes and weights (used as coins of different denominations) were guaranteed by the state with punch-marks of tokens (images of kings, etc.) on one side and letters indicating value and the office of issue on the other side. By the seventh century B. C., regular coinage of gold, silver, lead and various alloys came into use. Coins at this stage used to be minted by dies and cast (Barnett, 1977, pp. 230-31; U. N. Ghosal, 1976, Ch-VIII, pp. 279-80, Kosambi, 1981, pp. 124-25). Barnett opines that Achaemenid and Greek influences played an important role in evolution of coinage in India at this stage.

Various coins as mentioned in Arthaśāstra were:

Silver pana with its subdivisions was the standard coin. Copper māṣaka with its subdivisions was the token currency.

Exchange rate:

One pana (Karsapana) = 16 masakas

Subdivisions of pana:

1, 1/2., ¼ and $1/8^{th}$.

Subdivisions of māṣaka:

1 and ½

¼ māṣaka = 1 kakani

$1/8^{th}$ māṣaka = ½ kakani

(Book-II, ch-12)

Thus it appears that the coins in use were (in ascending order of value):

½ kakani, 1 kakani (= $1/4^{th}$ māṣaka); ½ māṣaka;

1 masaka (1/16 pana), 1/8 pana; ¼ pana; ½ pana and 1 pana.

Arthaśāstra also mentions gold coins (Book-II, ch-14), but it may be presumed that they were not in use in regular exchange. Moreover, the rate of exchange of these coins with other coins is not also clear. From Arthaśāstra, it appears that coins were to be minted by the state under the strict supervision of the state Gold Smith. But there are also indications that in certain conditions, private persons were permitted to mint silver coins. To quote from Arthaśāstra: "For minting coins (for private parties) he should charge a duty of eight percent, surcharge of five per cent....." (Chunder, 1995, p. 125).

2.4.2. Banking

With the development of trade and transactions among merchants on credit, there was considerable development of credit instruments; and banks, performing the twin functions of receiving deposits and lending money, emerged. Generally craft and trade guilds used to perform banking functions (A. N. Bose, 1945, vol-II, p. 348; Mookerji in Majumdar, ed, 1980, p. 601). There is, however, no evidence of development of bank credit to the extent that can affect money supply perceptively and, thereby, create problems in the price front.

2.5. Fiscal Policy and Public Finance

In ancient India, fiscal policy of the government aimed at maintaining a surplus budget and, at the worst, a balanced budget. So unlike in modern states, deliberate fiscal and budgetary deficits, generating problems in the price front, were completely unlikely in ancient India. Thus fiscal measures for price control, unlike in modern states, had very little relevance in ancient India. In fact, in ancient India, existence of deficit in state finance and public borrowing were looked upon as weakness of the government. According to Aiyanger (1949, pp. 162-64) ancient Indian financial methods differed from modern methods as in the former, because of limited sources of revenue (printing of paper currency was unknown in those days and borrowing was considered to be inimical to sound finance), state expenditure could never be permitted to exceed the revenue received. Aiyanger remarks in this connection: "The rigorous persistence by states, in the policy of securing surpluses is a normal feature of Indian Cameralism (Ibid. p. 164). Kauṭilya also subscribed to this ancient Indian view as would be clear from the following subsection.

2.5.1. Fiscal Policy in Arthaśāstra

In Arthaśāstra, Kauṭilya warns against fiscal deficits: "For, a king with a small treasury swallows up the citizens and the country people themselves" (2/1/16). Kauṭilya defines the best treasury as: "Acquired lawfully by the ancestors or by oneself, consisting mostly of gold and silver, containing various kinds of big jewels and cash, (one) that would withstand a calamity even of a long duration in which there is no in-come,—these are the excellences of a treasury" (6/1/10).

In many other instances Kauṭilya refers, directly or indirectly to the necessity of a surplus budget (2/6, 7, 8, 9, 16; 5/3; 8/1).

Kauṭilya also prescribes various exceptional measures (sometimes even unethical) for replenishment of treasury in case of crisis (5/2). Thus we see that Arthaśāstra fiscal policy, opting to maintain a surplus budget, was not likely to generate any problem for the price front.

Now, let us look into the source of revenue and heads of expenditure of the state and their relevance for Arthaśāstra price policy.

2.5.2. Sources of Revenue

As regards sources of revenue of the state, Kauṭilya recommends (2/6/1) "The Administrator should attend to the fort, the country, mines, irrigation works, forests, herds and trade-routes (as the main sources of revenue)."

The Heads of Revenue were (2/6/10):

"Price, share, surcharge, monopoly tax, fixed tax, manufacturing charge and penalty constitute the heads of income."

As regards collection of tolls at the entrance of each urban centre (sthaniya, droṇemukha, etc.) the following guidelines are given in the text:

2/21/1: The Collector of Customs and Tolls should establish the customs house and the flag facing the east or the north in the vicinity of the big gates (of the city).

2/21/2: The receivers of duty, four or five in number, should record in writing (details about) traders who have arrived in a caravan, who they are, from what place, with how much merchandise and where the identity-pass (was issued) or the stamping was made.

All the commodities entering the urban centres should bear the official seals of the place of origin. False statement by merchants as regards quantity, quality, price, etc. was not possible because of exhaustive espionage network.

3 For (goods) without the stamp the penalty is double the dues.

4 For those with a forged stamp, the fine is eight times the duty.

5 For those with broken stamps, the penalty is distraint in the ware-house.

6 In case of change of the royal stamp or of (change in) the name, he should make (the trader) pay a fine of one pana and a quarter per load.

7 Traders shall declare the quantity and price of the goods that have arrived at the foot of the flag, 'Who is willing to purchase these goods, so much in quantity, at this price?'

8 When it has been thrice proclaimed, he should give it to those who have sought it.

9 In case of competition among purchasers, the increase in price together with the duty shall go to the treasury.

10 If for fear of duty a (trader) declares the quantity of the goods or the price to be less (than it actually is), the king shall confiscate that excess.

11 Or, the (trader) shall pay eight times the duty.

12 He should impose the same (penalty) in case of depreciation of price of a package containing

goods by (showing) a sample of lower value and in case of concealment of goods of high value by goods of low value.

13 Or, if through fear of a rival purchaser a (trader) increases the price beyond the (due) price of a commodity, the king shall receive the increase in price, or make the amount of duty double.

14 The same (penalty) eightfold (shall be imposed) on the Superintendent concealing (the trader's offences).

15 Therefore, the sale of goods should be made by weighing, measuring or counting; an appraisal (of value should be made) of goods of small value and goods enjoying concessions.

16 And for goods that have passed beyond the foot of the flag without the duty being paid, the fine is eight times the duty.

17 Secret agents operating on roads and in places without roads should find out such (evasion).

18 Goods intended for marriage, marriage-gifts accompanying the bride, goods intended as gifts, goods required on the occasion of a sacrifice or a ceremony or a birth and goods used in various rituals like worship of the gods, tonsure rite, initiation for Veda study, hair-cutting rite, consecration for a vow and so on, should go duty-free.

19 For a (person) making a false declaration (in this respect) the punishment for theft (shall be imposed).

20 For the trader taking out a commodity for which duty has not been paid along with one for which duty has been paid, or carrying off a second (commodity) under one stamp after breaking open the package, forfeiture of the same and an equal amount as fine (shall be the punishment). 21 For the (trader) carrying off (goods of high value) from the customs house after securing acceptance of cowdung (cakes) or straw as the basis (for calculating duty), the highest fine for violence (shall be the punishment).

It appears from above and other references scattered in various chapters of Arthaśāstra that the major sources of revenue of the government were:

i) State Sector production and share (rent) on production of state owned agricultural land, mines, etc. leased out to private persons (all in kind); income from services provided by the state (ferry charges etc.).

ii) Fines, fees, tributes etc.

iii) Commodity taxes and surcharges (vyaji).

iv) Taxes on household property.

The type of taxes and tax rates are not, however, clearly defined. There are also no clear information as regards the cases and rates of surcharges. Nevertheless, from Book-II, chs-6 & 21 and other scattered references in other chapters of Arthaśāstra, we may define two major types of commodity taxes:

i) Taxes on commodities while sold to traders by the producers (commodities cannot be sold directly to final users at the place of origin). We shall call these 'Production Taxes' which are to be added to production cost while determining prices of goods sold at local markets (i.e. market places of the town or village where the goods are produced).

ii) Tolls or entry taxes for commodities entering from outside (foreign lands, other cities and towns of rural areas) into an urban area (major cities, sthaniya, droṇemukha, khārvāṭika or saṅgrahana). Arthaśāstra recommends tax concessions to foreign goods. But information in this regard is scanty. So, in our closed economy model, we ignore this aspect. As the context of vyaji (surcharge) is not clear we also ignore that 4. Taxes are imposed as percentage of pretax price. For sake of simplicity, we assume that the rate of production tax for a commodity of local origin and the toll tax for the same commodity of outside origin is the same. The above simplifications may be changed by inclusion of complicated aspects (if information and data are available) without affecting the essential aspects of the model.

2.5.3. Heads of Expenditure

Although this aspect has very little relevance for our price control model, it may be briefly mentioned as concomitants to the revenue aspect. According to Arthaśāstra, the major heads of expenditure of the government were expenses for:

i) The Royal Family.

ii) Maintenance of state undertakings and public properties, internal administration and international relations.

iii) Defence.

2.6. Conclusion

The basic features of the Arthaśāstra economy as discussed above give us the following guidelines for our present study:

i) In the dual economic system, only the small but well organized sector has direct relevance for our price model.

ii) Highly developed conditions of trade and transport system in the organized sector make a well integrated price policy feasible.

iii) We assume (depending on the conditions of production prevalent during the relevant period) fixed coefficient technologies and constant returns to scale for processing of commodities in the urban sector. So, aij (the amount of the ith product required to produce one unit of the jth product) is constant for all levels of output and at all industrial units for any particular pair i and j.

iv) Price of a commodity at the local market (market of the town where the commodity is produced) includes only production tax, but the price of a commodity of outside origin includes two taxes; production tax at the place of origin and entry tax at the toll-gate.

v) Monetary and fiscal policies were not required for price control. So, only direct control measures are relevant for our study.

vi) For sake of simplicity and because of lack of adequate information, we consider a closed economy model, ignore surcharges and assume the same rate for production tax and entry tax for a particular commodity.

vii) With no loss of generality, transport costs for commodities sold at local markets may be ignored. For commodities of distant origin, transport cost varies directly as distance of the place of origin. (Here by transport cost, we mean the composite cost which includes, besides direct transportation expenses, expenses for security, storage etc. and all other costs in transit)5.

viii) We use as monetary unit, the copper pana (or karsapana). To avoid complications, use of various subdivisions of pana in which coins of smaller subdivisions were minted in those days and also the copper māṣ aka and its subdivisions are avoided. In fact, in our hypothetical accounting model, actual names of smaller monetary units do not have any special significance. We use, instead of following the practice in Arthaśāstra (1/2, ¼, 1/8, 1/16, 1/32, 1/64, 1/128 divisions of pana as the accounting units), the subdivision of pana as in the case of sub-divisions of the Rupee into paises. This is not going to affect the basic aspect of our analysis.

In the Appendix to this chapter, we provide a list of various commodities mentioned in different chapters of Arthaśāstra. Names of many commodities are obscure (either they are no longer available now a days or the equivalent modern interpretation has not been possible). Effort has been made to make the list exhaustive.

The commodities have been classified into three categories as follows:

i) Primary commodities: Agricultural products, forest products, raw mineral ores, goods collected from sea, forests, etc. before processing and refinement.

ii) Simple products: Commodities produced by simple processing like extraction of minerals from ores, extraction of oil from oil seeds, spinning of threads from raw cotton etc.

iii) Advanced products: Commodities produced by at least two-step processing from the primary stage, e.g. weaving, manufacturing metallic pots etc. To avoid confusion, it should be mentioned that this is an arbitrary classification exclusively meant for our model and has got nothing to do with the Marxian or any other conventional classification.

Chapter-3: Production Structure in Arthaśāstra

3.1: Introduction

Study of Arthaśāstra reveals that in that period production was carried on in both the state sector and the private sector. In many cases, there were state monopolies with very limited scope for private production. In certain cases, state properties were leased out to private producers on the basis of a fixed proportion of output (bhāga) paid to the state. In certain cases, both state production and private production (with private ownership) existed side by side. It appears that all the commodities, mentioned in Appendices to the second chapter, were produced in the state sector. Total state owned products (direct state production plus shares from private lessees) were utilized to fill the buffer stock requirements of the state storehouse (determined by the state policy on the basis of present needs and anticipated future requirements). Outputs over and above these requirements were sold to the private sector.

In many cases, scope for private sector production was limited (either nil or not enough to meet consumption and input requirements). In these cases, private sector had to depend on state sector sales to meet consumption and input requirements. The commodities produced in both the sectors are divided (as discussed in chapter-2) into three major categories. Production structure in each sector depends on the amounts of production of different categories and the technical relations among them. The role of traders, who undertook to circulate commodities throughout the country, is very important in establishing the relations between the state sector and the private sector, among production units and between producers and consumers. So in the analysis of the production structure in Arthaśāstra, discussion of trading activities automatically comes up.

The state had semi-monopolistic control over the transport system, although it is nowhere indicated that private persons were not permitted to carry on transportation business. But, because of the dominance of the state sector in this field, various transportation charges, which enter into prices, were likely to be determined by the state.

Now we take up the features of production structure in the state sector and the private sector in the following two sections.

3.2: Production Structure in the State Sector

We have already mentioned that the state sector in Arthaśāstra used to produce all the commodities required for state sector consumption, input use and replenishment of buffer stock. It appears that direct state production and shares (bhāgas) obtained from leases of state property could meet total state sector requirements of each commodity. Now we take up the state sector production in primary and secondary (simple products and advanced products) categories and establish the technical relation among different products.

3.2.1: State Sector Primary Products

This category includes (as specified in chapter-2) agriculture, oceanic and forest products and exploration of mineral ores. We take up each item one by one.

1) Agriculture: In Arthaśāstra economy, the state had ownership over a vast amount of agricultural land although (as we shall discuss in subsequent sections) there was no state monopoly over agricultural land holding. State-owned land may be divided into two major categories: crown or sitā land which was cultivated directly by the state (by employing labourers) and state owned land leased out to private cultivators.

As regards the cultivation of crown land, the direction given in Arthaśāstra (Book-2, chap-24) are:

2/24/2: He should cause them to be sown in land, suitable for each, which has been ploughed many times, through serfs, labourers and persons paying off their fines by personal labour.

2/24/3: And he should cause no delay in (the work of) these on account of ploughing machines, implements and bullocks, and on account of (the work of) artisans, such as smiths, carpenters, basket-makers, rope-makers, snake-catchers and others.

So, we find that a part of state owned land was cultivated by the state itself. The rest of state owned land was leased out to share croppers on the basis of payment of rent (mainly in kind). The terms and conditions of the lease becomes clear from the following excerpts from Arthaśāstra:

2/1/8 He should allot to tax-payers arable fields for life.

9 Un-arable fields should not be taken away from those who are making them arable.

10 He should take away (fields) from those who do not till them and give them to others.

11 Or, village servants and traders should till them.

12 Or, those who do not till should make good the loss (to the treasury).

13. And he should favour them with grains, cattle and money.

14 These they should pay back afterwards at their convenience.

15 And he should grant to them favours and exemptions which would cause an increase in the treasury, (but) avoid such as would cause loss to the treasury.

Thus it is seen that agricultural output at the command of the state sector consisted of products of crown land and taxes (rent in kind) received from the lease holders of state owned land.

2) Forest, Animal, Oceanic and Mineral Products

Arthaśāstra prescribed state monopoly over all natural forests and all forest products, all wild animals and animal products and all oceanic products (as listed respectively in Appendices A(i), A(ii) and A(iii) of chapter-2). This is evident from the following excerpts from Arthaśāstra:

2/2/5: And he should establish forests, one each for the products indicated as forest produce, as well as factories for goods made from forest produce, and (settle) foresters, attached to the produce-forests.

2/12/27 The Superintendent of Mines should establish factories for (articles of) conch-shells, diamonds, gems, pearls, corals and caustics as well as commerce in them.

Arthaśāstra prescribes state monopoly over all mines containing metals and precious stones (listed in Appendix A-ii in chapter-2), but state itself did not operate all the mines. Some of them were leased out to private persons. To quote:

2/12/22 He should let for part-share or on lease a mine that is burden-some in point of expenses or working; a light one, he should work himself.

Thus we see that state sector output of forest, mineral and oceanic products consisted of state's own collection and extraction of these products and share of salt and mineral ores for mines leased out. It appears that the scope of private sector production was very limited in these fields. So we assume that most of these products needed for input and consumption requirements of the private sector had to be purchased from the state.

Benoy Chandra Sen's observations (1967, p. 10) in this regard are worth mentioning: " the state in Kauṭilya has a complete monopoly over mines , which, if properly worked and managed, can place at its disposal the types of wealth to which a special significance is attached without any ambiguity .... Mines can be worked either directly by the state under its own management, or by private bodies under a licence issued by the Government in exchange for a stipulated number of shares in the business, probably of the output only or some kind of charge of Royalty."

3.2.2. State Sector Simple Products

Commodities produced by simple processing fall in this category. They include first stage processing of agriculture, forestry and animal based products, extraction of minerals from ores etc. the detailed list of these commodities is given in Appendix B of chapter-2. Some examples are:

Agriculture based products: Acids from grains, Cotton threads, Flour.

Forest based products: Charcoal, Rope, Sap of plants, Boards, Wooden vessel to keep oil.

Animal based products: Butter, Leather, Powder of bones, horns etc.

Metal based products: Extraction of various metals from ores, Purification and testing of metals, Alloys of metals, Building materials.

Most of these commodities were produced in the state sector2. But the private sector was also permitted to produce these commodities. The state enjoyed exclusive monopoly power over the production of liquor and other intoxicants which are mainly agriculture and forest based simple products. Only on special occasions and festivals, private persons were permitted to manufacture liquor for a period specified by the state. To quote:

2/25/1: The Controller of Spirituous Liquors should cause trade in wines and ferments to be carried on in the fort, the country of the camp, through persons dealing in wines and ferments, being born to that work, either in one place or in many places or according to (convenience for) purchase and sale.

2/25/2: He should fix six hundred panas as the penalty for those who manufacture, purchase or sell in other places.

2/25/35: Householders should be free to manufacture white liquor on festive occasions or an arista for medicinal use, or other (spirituous preparations).

2/25/36: On the occasions of festivals, gatherings and fairs, permission to manufacture and sell liquor should be granted for four days.

2/25/37: On those days, he should charge a penalty per day from those not permitted, till the end of the festivity.

A close look at the list of the commodities in this category reveals that most of them required only primary products as variable inputs. They could be produced simply by applying labour (pressing, grinding, drying, frying, burning, decocting, cutting etc.) on primary products. Some of them were mixtures of primary products and some simple products (e.g. liquors, astringents etc.) and some were mixtures of some simple products (e.g. alloys of some metals). Metal extractions required both primary products (bile, urine, cowdung etc.) and simple products (acids, alkalis etc.) (Book-2: chs-15, 17 and 25).

In most of the cases input requirement is unidirectional, i.e. if aij (the amount the ith simple product required to produce one unit of the jth simple product) is positive then aji is zero for the same I and j. it is also clear that aij = 0 for I = j, i.e. no commodity is required to produce itself. Many commodities are not interdependent, so that for many pairs of I and j, both aij and aji are zero.

Production of these goods required fixed capital gods which are produced mostly in the advanced processing sector. Some simple contrivances like boards, baskets, earthenware etc. were produced mostly in the simple processing sector itself. They include: Bamboo mats, Boards, Boxes, Brooms, Grain baskets, Ladder, Net, Wooden planks, Earthen pots and vessels, Millstone (rochani), Winnowing fans, Wooden contrivances for rice pounding. This list is almost exhaustive (available from Arthaśāstra).

3.2.3. State Sector Advanced Products

This category includes the following products:

1. Building and construction

2. Coins made of gold, silver, copper and alloys

3. Weaving

4. Ornaments

5. Vehicles

6. Arms and weapons

7. Glass

8. Shoes and other leather products

9. Metallic pots and utensils

10. Umbrellas

11. Surgical instruments

12. General instruments used as capital goods (Appendix B-II, 3(a) to chapter-2)

13. Variable inputs (Appendix B-II, 4 to chapter-2)

Most of the commodities produced in this category are final consumption goods. Items under 12 are fixed capital goods and those under 13 are variable inputs required for production in other sectors.

In the advanced category the state used to enjoy monopoly power as regards the production of (i) Coins, (ii) Vehicles, Arms and Ammunitions, Weights and Measures.

i) Coins: The state used to enjoy monopoly power over the production of coins (Book-2, ch-12), but in certain cases private persons were permitted to produce coins under strict regulation by the state. This would be evident from the following excerpt from Arthaśāstra:

2/12/26: (He should also fix) a coining fee of eight per cent, a commission of five per cent, an inspection fee of one-eighteen per cent, and a penalty of twenty-five panas for those who manufacture, purchase, sell and examine in other places.

From the above quotation it becomes clear that private persons could mint coins only in areas and workshops specified by the state.

ii) Vehicles etc.: It appears from prescriptions in Arthaśāstra (Book-2, chs-18, 19, 33) that the state used to produce weights and measures, all categories of vehicles and arms and ammunitions. But there is no categorical statement that private persons would not be permitted to manufacture these commodities. In fact, we cannot call this exclusive monopoly of the state. To be more exact, production in these categories was mainly the concern of the state and the scope of private production was very limited.

As regards other products where state and private sectors had equal importance, Arthaśāstra (Book-2, ch-23) gives details of state sector weaving activities (it may be presumed that in many respect similar methods were adopted in other major advanced production in the state sector).

The state used to employ skilled artisans for weaving, while for spinning yarns (a primary process) required for weaving the state used to employ widows, disabled women, maids, female mendicants, women working in lieu of punishment, aged prostitutes, etc. Respectable women, who did not come out of home, were also given contract for spinning yarn at home.

3.2.4: State Sector Services

In this category two major items are: i) Transport and ii) Trade

i) Transport

Prescription in Arthaśāstra and other evidences show that there was partial socialization of transport services. It appears , however, that there was no restriction on private transport services which mainly consisted of transportation by carts, travelling chariots, ships, boats, canoes etc. As regards water transport, the state had exclusive ownership of water routes in oceans (off shore), rivers etc. There were state ferry services. Ferry charges for men, animals and goods of various kinds along with cases of concessions and exemptions are specified in Arthaśāstra (Book-2, ch-28). Private persons could use the water routes by paying appropriate fees. Sometimes fixed taxes were levied for using waterways irrespective of the frequency of use. Merchants and other private persons could use their own boats or ships by paying requisite fees for the use of water ways. State-owned ships and boats were also lent to private persons for personal as well as commercial purposes.

2/28/1-27

1: The Controller of Shipping should look after activities concerning sea voyages and ferries at the mouths of rivers, as well as ferries over natural lakes, artificial lakes and rivers, in the sthaniya and other (towns).

2: Villages on their shores and banks shall pay a fixed (tax).

3: Fishermen shall pay one-sixth (of their catch) as rent for the boats.

4 Traders shall pay a part (of the goods) as duty according as it may be current at the ports, those travelling by the king's ships (shall pay) hire for the voyage.

5 Those fishing for conch-shells and pearls shall pay a rent for the boats, or sail in their own boats.

6 And (the duty of) the Supervisor of these is explained by (that of) the Superintendent of Mines.

7 The Controller of Shipping shall observe the regulations in a port town as fixed by the Commissioner of Ports.

8 He should rescue boats that have gone out of their course or are tossed about by a gale, like a father.

9 He should make goods that have fallen in water either duty-free or pay half the duty.

10 And he should send these (boats) on, as commissioned, at times suitable for voyage from the port.

11 He should demand duty from ships sailing on sea when they come within the domain.

12 He should destroy (boats) that cause harm, also those coming over from the enemy's territory and those violating the regulations of the port.

13. And he should keep in use big boats in charge of a captain, a pilot, a manipulator of the cutter and ropes and a bailer of water, on

big rivers that have to be ferried on (even) in winter and summer, small ones on small rivers flowing (only) in the rainy season.

14 And these should have their crossing places fixed because of the danger of crossing by traitorous persons.

15 For one crossing out of time or elsewhere than at the crossing, (the punishment shall be) the lowest fine for violence.

16 For one who crosses without authority even at the proper time and at the crossing, the

penalty for crossing is twenty-six panas and three quarters.

17 'There shall be no penalty for fishermen, (carriers of) loads of wood and grass, attendants

at flower-gardens, fruit-orchards and vegetable gardens and cowherds, also for those whose going after an envoy is conceivable, and for those carrying out activity in connection with goods for the army, when these cross in their own barges, as well as for those who ferry across seeds, food-stuffs and articles for household use in villages along the water-courses.

18 Brahmins, wandering monks, children, old persons, sick persons, carriers of royal edicts and pregnant women should cross with a sealed pass from the Controller of Shipping.

19 Persons from foreign lands may enter when permission to enter is granted or on the testimony of the caravan.

20 He should cause to be arrested a person carrying off the wife, the daughter or the property of another, a person who is frightened or agitated, a person hiding behind a heavy load, a person concealing (his face) by a load on the head containing heavy goods, a wandering monk who has just put on the marks or who is without the marks, a person whose illness cannot be seen, a person showing a changed appearance because of fear, a person secretly carrying goods of high value, letters, weapons or means of fire, a person with poison in hand, a person who has travelled a long distance and a person without a sealed pass.

21 A small animal and a man with a load (in hand) shall pay one masaka, a load on the head, a load on the back, a cow and a horse (shall pay) two (masakas), a camel and a buffalo four, a small vehicle five, one driven by bullocks six, a cart seven, a load of commodities one quarter (of a pana).

22 By that is explained (fare for) a load of goods.

23 The fare for ferries on big rivers is double.

24 Villages on water-ways shall pay a fixed amount of food and wages (for the ferrymen).

25 At the frontiers, ferrymen should recover the duty, the escort-charges and the road cess, and should confiscate the goods of one going out without a seal, also (those) of a person crossing with a heavy load at an improper time and elsewhere than at the regular crossing.

26 When a boat, that is lacking in men or equipment or is unseaworthy, comes to grief, the Controller of Shipping shall make good what is lost or ruined.

27 Between the eighth day after the full moon day of Asadha and that of Kartika, ferrying (shall be provided). The workman should give a surety and should bring in the regular daily earnings.

It becomes clear that because of the dominance of the state sector in transport services, transport charges were mainly determined by the state sector.

ii) Trade:

Many commodities produced in the state sector were sold to the private sector for consumption and use as inputs. This happened mostly in cases where scope of production in the private sector was limited and therefore, not adequate to meet consumption and input requirements. They mostly included primary products (forest, oceanic and animal products, and mineral ores), salts, liquor and narcotics, weights and measures, precious stones etc.

These commodities were not sold directly to the final users but they were sold to the traders who carried the commodities to different corners of the country and sold at specified markets to final users (2/12). Sometimes the state used to employ retail sellers on payment of fixed commissions to sell state sector commodities directly to the final users (2/16). It appears from the study of Arthaśāstra that the task of countrywide circulation of state sector commodities (allotted for sales to the private sector) fell mostly on private traders. But they had to strictly adhere to the guidelines imposed by the state.

3.3. Production Structure in the Private Sector

As in the state sector, private sector production is also divided into primary production and two categories of secondary production, viz. simple production and advanced production. It is evident from the study of Arthaśāstra and other writings on the period3, that in the primary sector, excepting agriculture, there was almost exclusive state monopoly over all the fields and private sector had to depend for non-agricultural primary inputs and consumption goods on the sales of the state sector. As regards secondary production, many authors opine that scope of private sector production was very insignificant. A close study of Arthaśāstra and the relevant period, however, does not corroborate this view. Private sector services, especially trading, is very important in our context as the private trading class acted as the blood-stream of the economy by circulating commodities between the state sector and the private sector, between private producers and users (as consumption goods or inputs) of commodities and economically linking the vast geographical area of the country. In the following subsections we are going to discuss the characteristics of each of the above categories of production in the private sector and the technical relationships among them.

3.3.1. Private Sector Primary Products

Among the primary products only three categories of goods could be produced in the private sector, viz. i) Exploration of mineral ores,

ii) Agricultural products and iii) Products from domestic animals. As regards other products, e.g. forest and oceanic products, products from wild animals etc., the state used to enjoy exclusive monopoly power.

i) Mining:

Private ownership of mines was not permitted. But some of the state owned mines, viz. the ones containing inferior grades of ores and involving very high operational costs were leased out to private producers. Salt production (both mineral and oceanic) rights were leased out to private persons in lieu of rents, taxes and surcharges (chapter-3, section 3.2.1. of this study). It may be presumed that private production in this category, after payment of the stipulated share (bhāga) to the state, was not adequate to meet the requirements of the private sector. So, for these products, private consumers and input users had to depend mainly on the sales of the state sector.

ii) Agriculture

Private sector agricultural production may be divided into two major categories:

a) Share cropping on state-owned land leased out to private cultivators

b) Cultivation on privately-owned land

a) Share cropping

It is found from Arthaśāstra that state-owned land was, in many cases, distributed to private cultivators (2/1) the period of lease covering the life span of the cultivators on condition of cultivating the land in proper manner and regular payment of the stipulated rent.

2/1/10: He should take away (fields) from those who do not till them and give them to others.

b) Cultivation of privately-owned land

Many authors opine that besides share-cultivation on state-owned land, there did not exist any private ownership of land in the true sense of the term in the age of Arthaśāstra. In fact Book-2 of Arthaśāstra, where most of the economic matters are dealt with, does not make any mention of privately-owned land. Nevertheless, evidence (although indirect) of private ownership of land is to be found in some parts of Arthaśāstra, e.g. in Book-3, chapter-9, the question of the existence of private ownership of agricultural land came up several times in connection with different legal provisions. A few such cases are cited below:

3/9/1 Kinsmen, neighbours and creditors, in this order, shall have the right to purchase landed property (on sale).

2 After that, others who are outsiders (may bid for purchase).

3 (Owners) shall proclaim a dwelling (as for sale) in front of the house, in the presence of members of forty neighbouring families, and a field, a park, an embankment, a tank or a reservoir (as for sale) at the boundaries, in the presence of village elders who are neighbours, according to the extent of the boundary, saying 'at this price who is willing to purchase?'

4 What has been thrice proclaimed and not objected to, the purchaser shall be entitled to purchase.

There are also evidence that private land was, in many cases, leased out to share cultivators, e.g.

3/9/33 When tanks and embankments are newly constructed, an exemption (from taxes) for five years (should be granted), when those that are ruined and abandoned are renovated, an exemption for four years, when those that are over-grown with weeds are cleared, for three years, when dry land is newly brought under cultivation, for two years.

34 He is free to mortgage or sell.

35 (Owners) may give (water) in return for a share of produce of various kinds from sowings in fields, parks and gardens watered by (their) dug-out

36 And those who use these on lease, on hire, as a pledge, for a share or with authorization for use, shall keep (them) in-repair.

37 In case of failure to repair, the fine in double the loss.

38 For one letting out water from the dams out of turn, the fine shall be six panas, also for one obstructing, through negligence, the water of others when it is their turn.

A close study of Arthaśāstra makes the impression that the major portion of agricultural land in the country was privately owned and cultivated. The government claimed ownership of agricultural land belonging to the newly constructed villages. Even in this case, a large part of state-owned land was leased out to private cultivators (2/1; 3/9). So, except in the case of crown land cultivated directly by the state, agricultural activities were mostly carried on in the private sector. Thus it may be presumed that production on privately owned land and shares from privately cultivated state-owned land (after payment of state's share) could meet private sector requirements of agricultural products.

iii) Domestic Animals

Primary animal products like milk, bone, horn, hoof, dung and urine of animals, fat, bile, raw hide etc. could be procured from private animal husbandry. State had monopoly over wild beasts, elephants etc. So, animal products like ivory, skins of wild animals, etc. had to be purchased from the state.

3.3.2. Private Sector Secondary Products

(Simple and Advanced Processes)

As Regards Secondary Productive Activities, the State Used to Enjoy Monopoly Power in Many Fields as Discussed in Section 3.2. Nevertheless, the private sector, too had scope for production in a large number of fields. For metal and mineral based industries, the private sector producers had to depend exclusively on state sector sales for raw materials as the state enjoyed monopoly power over metal and mineral exploration. Moreover, several restrictions were imposed on private producers in this field, e.g.

2/12/18: What is produced from ores, he should put to use in factories for the respective metals.

2/12/19: He should establish trade in manufactured goods in a single place, and (lay down) a penalty for those who manufacture, purchase or sell elsewhere.

According to some authors, scope of private sector secondary production was insignificant in the Arthaśāstra state. In this regard D. D. Kosambi observes, " perhaps the most serious of the restrictions on the manufacturing trader was the limit to his supply of skilled labour" (Kosambi, 1981, p. 156).

If by private sector production outside the craft guilds is considered, it was definitely insignificant. But private production means production both within and outside the guilds. And so, scope of private sector production (except in case of forest, mine and ocean based primary production) was not at all limited.

In fact, private sector secondary productivity in the Arthaśāstra state was chiefly by the powerful craft guilds.

Artisans with specialized skills used to carry on manufacturing activities in the private sector. Specialized skills became particularly necessary for the advanced industrial processes. These skills could be acquired by artisans through hereditary training. The simple processes, it may be presumed, did not require such specialized skills. Most of the artisans were organized under strong craft guilds which used to regulate the qualities of products, input specifications, prices and other matters associated with production and marketing of craft guilds. They also used to help the artisans by providing raw materials, marketing facilities, etc. Many authors have discussed, in detail, the vast coverage of industrial activities of the guilds (M. A. Buch, 1979, pp. 116-236). The major industries under craft guilds have been mentioned in chapter 2 (section 2.2.2.) of this study.

One important conclusion that can be drawn from all evidences is that private manufacturing in the age of Arthaśāstra were carried on mostly by the artisans organized under strong guilds. Scope of manufacturing activities outside the guilds was indeed limited. But this does not, in any sense, imply that the scope of private sector manufacturing activities, as such, was limited.

3.3.3. Private Services

In Arthaśāstra, there are mentions of washermen, musicians, physicians and several minor professionals and craftsmen belonging to the services sector (4/1 and scattered in many other chapters). Banking activities were organized by the guilds (Bose, 1945, p. 348 and Mookerji, in Majumdar (ed), 1980, p. 601). We have already discussed in section 3.2 that transport was partly socialized and scope of the private sector was very limited in this sphere. In fact, the most important service sector activity in the private sector was trade

Private Sector Trade

Traders and merchants, like the circulation of blood, used to interconnect all segments of and all sorts of productive activities of the entire economy. They used to supply raw materials, intermediates and implements necessary for all sorts of private sector production and used to market the final products. According to Arthaśāstra principles:

2/22/9: And no sale of commodities (shall be allowed) in the places of their origin.

In this connection, Kosambi remarks (1982, p. 155):

"This implies that the purchased material had to be processed in some way, and generally to be transported to a distant place. The trader had to add value by manufacture, or by transport. The latter was most important in keeping the circulation of goods and money at a satisfactory level."

This interpretation appears to be an exaggeration of the view expressed in the text. A straight forward and meaningful interpretation is that the producers of commodities were not permitted to sell their products directly to the final users. This had to be done through the intermediation of the traders. The traders, in those days, used to play the role of brokers or commission agents in modern economics.

Kosambi is, however, right to point out that flow of commodities throughout the country was maintained by the traders.

Retail Sellers

It appears from scattered mentions in Arthaśāstra that middlemen and retail sellers, employed by the traders on commission, used to sell the consumer-goods to the final consumers. To quote from Arthaśāstra:

3/12/25: Concerning sale through agents, however, salesmen selling the commodity at the proper place and time shall pay (to the owner) the price as received and the profit.

3/12/26: Or, if (the price is) lower because of their missing the proper place and time, they shall pay the price according to the rate at the time of giving (the goods to them for sale) and the profit.

3/12/27: Or, if selling (the goods) as agreed upon they do not make a profit, they should pay only the price.

3/12/28: Or, if the price is lower because of a fall in prices, they should give the lower price as reduced.

3/12/29: Or, in the case of dealers, who are trustworthy and free from blame so far as the king is concerned, they may not pay even the price of what is lost or ruined through deterioration or a

sudden calamity.

3/12/30 But of commodities removed in space or time they shall pay the price and profit after deducting losses and expenses, and a separate share in the case of each of the different kinds of goods.

The essential guidelines that come out of the above quotations are:

i) Retail sellers are to be employed by traders on payment of daily wages (fixed by prior contract).

ii) Sales proceeds including profit are to be returned by the retail sellers to the traders who employ them.

iii) Any loss due to negligence of the retail sellers are to be borne by themselves.

3.4. Structure of Production in Compact Form

3.4.1. Basic Features and Assumptions

The production structure of the Arthaśāstra economy is decomposable like the simple 'Austrian Structure of Production' (DOSSOW, 1958, P. 255) in which some industries do not use as inputs the products of some other industries but the later use the products of the former as inputs. Classification of commodities in the Arthaśāstra economy reveals the following features:

1) Primary products (agricultural, mineral, forest and oceanic products) require labour as the only input. This is, in fact, a highly restrictive assumption as primary production requires threads, ropes, sacks, fertilizers, simple chemicals, metallic pots, boxes, ploughs and plough heads, sickles and many similar industrial products. Some of them are very simple and could be produced within the primary sector itself, but others are from the simple and advanced sectors. But considering the primitive nature of the primary sector (discussed in detail in chapter-2, under "dual economy"), it does not appear to be of much significance to incorporate this aspect in our mathematical model of production structure in Arthaśāstra.

2) Primary products are used as inputs for simple processes and for final consumption.

3) Simple products are used as inputs for both simple processes and advanced processes and for final consumption.

4) Advanced products are used as inputs for advanced processes and for final consumption.

5) In those days, simple processes required some instruments produced in the advanced processes. These instruments could be used for a long time, maintenance cost was insignificant and most of them could be repaired by the user himself. Nevertheless, we would incorporate the cost for fixed capital in simple processing and advanced processing as interest charges.

Our commodity classification is such that no advanced inputs, other than these instruments, were required for simple processing.

6) We have seen from our discussion of the production structure that the private sector was dependent on state sector sales of primary products except agricultural crops. It may be that the state used to sell some simple and advanced products to the private sector. But, for sake of simplicity, we assume for this model that private sector was self-sufficient as regards consumption and input requirements of simple and advanced products.

Relaxation of one or more of the above assumptions would simply make our model a little bit more complicated. But it would not change the basic nature of the model.

Now we are going to present the production structure discussed above with the help of an arithmetic example of [the Mathematical Model of Production Structure is given in the Appendix to this chapter].

3.5. Arithmetic Example of Production Structure

Let us consider a simple example with only six commodities:

$\underline{\mathbf{X}}_1$: agricultural product

X_2: non-agricultural primary product

$\mathbf{X}_3$ and $\mathbf{X}_4$: simple products

X_5 and X_6: advanced products

To distinguish different categories of products we use bold-underlined letters for agricultural products, italicized letters for non-agricultural primary products, bold letters for simple products and ordinary letters for the advanced products.

Technology and Input Coefficients

The preceding study reveals that in the Arthaśāstra economy, craft processing became mature, and technological specifications may therefore be assumed to be rigid. Let a_{ij} be the amount of the ith commodity required to produce one unit of the jth commodity. These coefficients are assumed to be the same for both the state sector and the private sector, and for all levels of output, i.e. we assume uniform technology for the entire economy and constant returns to scale. With these assumptions let us analyze the structure of production in the state sector for different categories of commodities.

According to the earlier assumption, primary production is very simple and need not require any sophisticated treatment. It has also been assumed that simple products require both primary products and other simple products as inputs, but primary products do not require simple products as inputs. In the same manner, advanced products require both simple products and other advanced products as inputs, but simple products do not require advanced products as inputs; advanced products do not require primary products as inputs and primary products do not require advanced products as inputs. Moreover, no product is required to produce itself. So, a_{11}, a_{22}, a_{33}, a_{44}, a_{55}, a_{66}, a_{15}, a_{16}, a_{31}, a_{32}, a_{41}, a_{42}, a_{51}, a_{52}, a_{53}, a_{54}, a_{61}, a_{62}, a_{63}, $a_{64} = 0$ by general assumption.

Now let the relevant non-zero coefficients for our simplified economy be:

$a_{13} = 0.2$, $a_{14} = 0$, $a_{23} = 0$, $a_{24} = 0.3$, $a_{34} = 0.3$, $a_{35} = 0.1$, $a_{36} = 0.2$, $a_{43} = 0.5$, $a_{45} = 0.2$, $a_{46} = 0.4$, $a_{56} = 0.5$, $a_{65} = 0.4$. The values of a_{12} and a_{21} are irrelevant, as we do not require any sophisticated treatment for the primary sector. $a_{14} = 0$ and $a_{23} = 0$, are not by general assumption, but for sake of simplicity; they could have been non-zero as well.

Interpretation: $a_{13} = 0.2$ means 0.2 units of X_1 is required to produce one unit of X_3 [e.g. to produce 1 Kg. of X_3, 200 grams of X_1 would be required]. All other coefficients may be treated in similar fashion.

With the above input specifications let us now find out the amount of production of different commodities in the state sector.

3.5.1. State Sector Production

Let the final demand for different commodities in the state sector be determined by prior state-policy and given as:

$C_1 = 100$; $C_2 = 100$; $C_3 = 31$; $C_4 = 44$; $C_5 = 100$; $C_6 = 200$.

Now let us start with the advanced products. Here:

Total demand for

X_5 = demand as input for X_6 + final consumption = $a_{56}X_6 + C_5$ = $0.5\,X_5 + 100$

Total demand for

X_6 = demand as input for X_5 + final consumption = $a_{65}\,X_5 + C_6$ = $0.4\,X_5 + 200$

Solving these equations we get: $X_5 = 250$ and $X_6 = 300$, i.e. to meet final demand requirements of 100 units of X_5 and 200 units of X_6, total production of these commodities should be respectively 250 and 300 units, i.e. 150 units and 100 units would respectively be used as inputs.

Simple Products

X_3 is required as inputs to produce X_4 and X_5 and for final demand. So

$X_3 = a_{34}X_4 + a_{35}X_5 + a_{36}X_6 + C_3 = 0.3X_4 + 0.1 \times 250 + 0.2 \times 300 + 31 = 0.3X_4 + 116$

Similarly

$X_4 = a_{43}X_3 + a_{45}X_5 + a_{46}X_6 + C_4 = 0.5X_3 + 0.2 \times 250 + 0.4 \times 300 + 44 = 0.5X_3 + 214$

Solving the above equations we get

$X_3 = 212$ units and $X_4 = 320$ units

Primary Products

Total demand for the first commodity:

$\underline{X_1} = \underline{a}_{13}X_3 + \underline{C_1} = 0.2 \times 212 + 100 = 142.4$ units

Total demand for the second commodity:

$X_2 = a_{24}X_4 + C_2 = 0.3 \times 320 + 100 = 196$ units

Thus to meet the final demand requirements:

$[\underline{C_1},\, C_2,\, C_3,\, C_4,\, C_5,\, C_6]$

= [100, 100, 31, 44, 100, 200] units, total amount of these commodities to be produced are:

[142, 196, 212, 320, 250, 300] units.

The amounts that could be produced in the simple and advanced sectors are dependent on production possibility in the primary sector. If 142 units of X_1 and 196 units of X_2 are not available from the primary sector, the final demand in one or more of the commodities are to be revised downwards. The commodities, whose production are to be revised downwards, are to be determined by the state on the basis of priorities and intensity of demand [requirements in the state sector].

The real-world economy, however, involves many more commodities in each section and there are many more interdependent and complicated relations. From the study of the Arthaśāstra of Kauṭilya, it appears that in the Arthaśāstra economy, a dynamically balanced production structure had already been achieved through the process of 'trial and error' and historical experience. With mathematical devices, the complicated relations could be solved within a short time, i.e. the production structure in the real Arthaśāstra economy could be approximated by a mathematical model.

3.5.2. Private Sector Production

For the private sector, it is meaningless to attempt to determine total demand for different kinds of commodities on the basis of given final demand [C] as in the state sector. Unlike the state sector, private sector did not have any central authority to determine final demand. In fact, production possibility and, thereby, consumption possibility in simple and advanced processing in the private sector was conditioned by private sector production of agricultural commodities and state sector sales of non-agricultural primary products to the private sector [determined by state policy]. For our simple example, we assume that the available primary products in the private sector are:

x_1 = 25 units (by private sector production)

x_2 = 40 units (by state sector sales

[We use lower case letters to denote private sector commodities]

Let direct consumption of these commodities in the private sector are respectively: 5 and 10 units. So available $\underline{x}_1$ for the production of x_3 and x_2 for the production of x_4 are respectively 20 and 30 units.

Now with 20 units of $\underline{x}_1$, amount of x_3 produced $= 20/\underline{a}_{13} = 20/0.2 = 100$ units.

Similarly, with given 30 units of x_2, amount of x_4 produced $= 30/a_{24} = 30/0.3 = 100$ units.

Again, the amount of x_3 required to produce 100 units of x_4 = $a_{34}x100 = 0.3x100 = 30$ units and the amount of x_4 required to produce 100 units of x_3 = $a_{43}x100 = 0.5x100 = 50$ units. So, $100 - 30 = 70$ units of x_3 and $100 - 50 = 50$ units of x_4 remains for final consumption and production of advanced products.

Let these 70 units of x_3 be divided by custom in the following manner:

40 units for direct consumption, 12 units as input to produce x_5, and 18 units as input to produce x_6. Similarly, available 50 units of x_4 be divided by custom as: 20, 10, 20.

Now to produce x_5, available x_3 and x_4 are respectively 12 and 10 units. With 12 units of x_3, amount of x_5 produced is $12/0.1 = 120$ units; but with 10 units of x_4, amount of x_5 produced is $10/0.2$ units $= 50$ units. So, maximum units of producible x_5 are 50 units only. Because of shortage of x_4, all available x_3 for production of x_5 cannot be utilized. To produce 50 units of x_5, amount of x_3 required is $50x0.1$ units $= 5$ units. So, the remaining $(12-5) = 7$ units of x_3 would remain unutilized.

Similarly, to produce x_6, available x_3 and x_4 are respectively 18 and 20 units. With these inputs, maximum amount of x_6 that could be produced is min $[18/0.2, 20/0.4]$ = min $[90, 50]$ = 50 units. Because of shortage of x_4, the maximum units of x_3 unutilized $= 50x0.2 = 10$ units, unutilized x_3 here are $(18-10) = 8$ units. Ultimately $(7 + 8) = 15$

units of unutilized (as input) x_3 are to be utilized as final consumption good or kept as reserve for the next period.

The matter, however, becomes complicated if we introduce a large number of commodities and large number of interdependent relations as in the real Arthaśāstra economy.

Chapter-4: Principles of Price Determination in Arthaśāstra

4.1. Introduction

Arthaśāstra state, like many other ancient states, used to impose strict state-control over prices of final commodities and factors of production. In fact, price policy was an integral part of of the Arthaśāstra economy. Perfect functioning of the Arthaśāstra economy depended on financial soundness of the government which again depended a good deal on revenue collected from commodity taxes. Uncertainty about prices of commodities would lead to uncertainty in the entire economic system as delineated in Arthaśāstra. So, a systematic and coherent price policy was a *sine qua non* for implementation of all other state policies as delineated in Arthaśāstra.

As regards the price policy in Arthaśāstra, the viewpoints of B. C. Sen and Altekar are worth mentioning. According to B. C. Sen (1967, pp. 28-29): "The principle, by which the state is to be guided, is not merely that profits and levies must be fully realized, but also that profiteering should be scaled down as far as possible, and prices so controlled that they may not affect the consumers adversely.

"A working idea of fair or proper price is behind the policy that governs trade and commerce. Price is not something dictated from above; it is determined by some imperative factors – such as cost, the exact ratio between demand and supply as far as ascertainable, fixed rates of profits, chargeable duty, etc. What is essential, however, is that the price, whatever it is, must be announced, offering little scope for haggling."

According to Altekar (1962, p. 327):

i) "It controlled retail and wholesale prices of commodities and tried to ensure their steady supply through its market superintendents."

ii) "It prohibited the entry of banned articles."

iii) "Products of state industries were offered by it to market."

The views mentioned above are corroborated by the policy prescriptions in Arthaśāstra as discussed below.

The exact mechanism of price control, however, has not been spelt out in detail in Arthaśāstra. Nevertheless, by piecing together the guideline scattered in various chapters of the book, we can get a fairly good insight into the actual mechanism of price control inherent in Arthaśāstra. In this chapter we endeavour to piece together various aspects of price control mechanism implicit in Arthaśāstra.

It should be mentioned in this connection that an integral part of price fixation in Arthaśāstra were the measures associated with its proper implementation. So we are to discuss these measures which made the price fixation policy in Arthaśāstra realistic and free from utopian degeneration. These measures included:

i) Administrative measures; ii) Espionage mechanism; iii) Accounting and iv) Buffer stock.

The short run and long run aspects of Arthaśāstra price policy are also of importance. All the above matters are discussed in detail in the following sections.

4.2. Determination of Prices of Goods and Services

The superintendent of commerce was entrusted with the task of enforcing the price policy. The prices of different commodities were to be fixed by him. He, however, did not fix prices arbitrarily. In fact, a uniform rule was followed throughout the country to determine the just prices of all the commodities. To quote from Arthaśāstra:

4/2/36: "In the case of commodities distant in place and time, however, the (Director of Trade), expert in fixing prices, shall fix the price after calculating the investment, the production of goods, duty, interest, rent and other expenses."

Thus,

Just Price = Average cost of production + Tolls and Taxes + Transport and associated costs + Profit margin.

Now, one may be tempted to compare this 'just price' with other similar concepts available in the jungle of modern economic literature. But a little reflection will make one realize that such comparisons do not make sense. There are innumerable normative approaches and value judgements as regards determination of 'fair price' or 'just price'. But in Arthaśāstra, 'just price' was simply a guideline that automatically came up from the general set up. It was, in fact, an integral part of the politico-economic system inherent in Arthaśāstra.

It is held by the author of Arthaśāstra that prices are to be so determined as to strike a balance between the interests of the buyers and that of the sellers. To fulfill this objective, the following guidelines are recommended by Arthaśāstra:

i) Goods are to be sold at places specified by the state and prices should be announced by the merchants:

2/21/7: Traders shall declare the quantity and price of the goods that have arrived at the foot of the flag, 'Who is willing to purchase these goods, so much in quantity, at this price?'

2/21/8: When it has been thrice proclaimed, he should give it to those who have sought it.

ii) Goods should bear official seal and properly weighed, measured and numbered. Violation of this rule was subject to punishment:

2/21/3-6: For (goods) without the stamp the penalty is double the dues.

For those with a forged stamp, the fine is eight times the duty.

For those with broken stamps, the penalty is distraint in the ware-house.

In case of change of the royal stamp or of (change in) the name, he should make (the trader) pay a fine of one pana and a quarter per load.

2/21/15: Therefore, the sale of goods should be made by weighing, measuring or counting; an appraisal (of value should be made) of goods of small value and goods enjoying concessions.

iii) Enhancement of price by bidding was discouraged:

2/21/9: In case of competition among purchasers, the increase in price together with the duty shall go to the treasury.

Thus we see that the buyers and sellers did not enjoy freedom as regards determination of prices. They had to accept the prices considered 'just' by the state.

We have already mentioned that according to Arthaśāstra principles,

Just price = Production cost + Tolls and Taxes + Transport and associated costs + Profit.

Now, production cost = Cost for raw materials + Wages + Interest.

In the subsequent sections we discuss in detail the principles of determination of different components of 'just price' as delineated in Arthaśāstra.

4.3. Wages

Guidelines for wage determination are scattered in chapters 12, 13, 14, 17 and 23 of Book-3, chapter 2 of Boo-4 and chapter 3 of Book-5 of Arthaśāstra. Principles for wage determination may be divided into two major categories: wages in the state sector and wages in the private sector.

4.3.1. Wages in the State Sector

Arthaśāstra gives a detailed list of the wages paid to different classes of state sector employees (Book-5, chapter-3/3-19). The table (see Appendix to this chapter) reveals that the highest wage (48,000: for Priest, Queen, Minister, Army Chief etc. was 800 times the lowest wage (60: for Bodyguards, Procurer of free labourers etc.). monetary units in which wages were calculated, are not, however, mentioned (so far as the available manuscript is concerned). In this regard, N. Śāstri (1967, p. 184) comments:

"These salaries are defined in the Arthaśāstra (V.3), but neither the unit of currency nor the period to which the figures relate is expressly stated."

From Arthaśāstra, it appears that sometimes state sector wages were paid in kind. The following excerpts from Arthaśāstra would corroborate this view:

i) 5/3/31: If he has a small treasury, he should give forest produce, cattle and fields and a little money.

ii) 3/3/34: Fixing one adhaka for a (servant with a) wage of sixty, he should fix food in accordance with the cash wage.

Other provisions for government employees were:

i) Higher incentives for higher skill and sincerity of the worker:

5/3/33: In this manner he should fix different (amounts of) food and wages for regular and casual servants according to their skill and work.

ii) Provisions for dependants of state employees who died while on duty:

5/3/28: Of those dying while on duty, the sons and wives shall receive the food and wages.

5/3/29: And their minor children, old and sick persons should be helped.

iii) Additional payments to state employees on occasions like funeral, sickness, child birth etc.

5/3/30: And he should grant them money and do honour on occasions of death, illness and birth ceremonials.

Besides the above principles regarding wages and salaries of state sector employees in administration, different chapters of Arthaśāstra mention the cases of employment of labourers and artisans for various types of productive activities (mining, various metal works, collection of forest products, spinning, weaving etc.) of the state sector, but there is no specific mention of the rates of wages to be paid. It is only indicated that in each case wages were to be determined on the basis of contract and in that context skill and sincerity would be considered as important factors in determining wage rates, e.g.

2/23/3: He should fix the wage after ascertaining the fineness, coarseness or medium quality of the yarn, and the largeness or smallness of quantity.

It appears that the state often utilized cheap and free labourers as is evident from the statements:

i) 2/23/2: He should get yarn spun out of wool, bark-fibres, cotton, silk-cotton, hemp and flax, through widows, crippled women, maidens, women who have left their homes and women paying off their fine by personal labour, through mothers of courtesans, through old female slaves of the king and through female slaves of temples whose service of the gods has ceased.

ii) 2/23/11: And those women who do not stir out — those living separately, widows, crippled women or maidens, — who wish to earn their living, should be given work by sending his own female slaves to them with (a view to) support (them).

iii) 2/24/2: He should cause them to be sown in land, suitable for each, which has been ploughed many times, through serfs, labourers and persons paying off their fines by personal labour.

The state also used to cultivate crown land ('sita) with free labourers (vishti) on payment of subsistence wages (Kosambi, 1981, pp. 150-51).

Arthaśāstra makes it clear that the terms and conditions of work-contract had to be strictly adhered to by the artisans and labourers employed on contract for state sector productive activities. Otherwise, wages would be deducted and /or fines imposed. This would be clear from the following excerpts from Arthaśāstra:

i) 2/14/2-4: They should do the work with the time and the (nature of the) work stipulated, without stipulation as to time when there is the excuse of the (nature of the) work.

In case the work is done otherwise (than as ordered) (there shall be) loss of wage and a fine double that (amount).

In case the time limit is exceeded, (he shall receive) a wage reduced by one-quarter and a fine double that (amount).

ii) 2/23/6: In case of diminution in yarn, (there shall be) a diminution in wage, according to the value of the stuff.

iii) 2/23/15: If a (woman) after receiving the wage does not carry out the work, he should make her forfeit the tongs formed by the thumb (and the middle finger), also those who have misappropriated or stolen and then run away.

iv) 2/23/16: And in the matter of wages, (there shall be) a fine for workmen in accordance with their offence.

Kauṭilya also mentions of various incentives to be provided by the state to the labourers in state sector productive activities so as to encourage them to produce more. Some of these incentives over and above contractual wages come to the fore from the following excerpts from Arthaśāstra:

i) 2/23/4-5: After finding out the amount of yarn, he should favour them with oil and myrobalan unguents.

And on festive days, they should be made to work by honouring (them) and making gifts.

ii) 2/23/8: And when starting mills for the weaving of (cloth from) ksauma, dukula, silk yarn, hair of the ranku deer, and cotton yarn, he should gratify the (workmen) by gifts of perfumes and flowers and by other means of showing good-will.

From the above discussion, the following salient features, as regards wage determination in the state sector, come out:

a) There were no specific wage rates. Wages were to be determined on the basis of contract for daily wages or for the amount of production.

b) The terms and conditions of work-contract were to be strictly adhered to by the employees. Otherwise, wages would be deducted and/or fines imposed.

c) Wages used to vary according to the skills of the labourers and the quality of the work done.

d) As regards determination of wages for different types of labourers, the decision of the state was final and the labourers had little bargaining power, except in the case of artisans belonging to guilds.

e) In many cases, the state was in an advantageous position to employ labourers at subsistence wages.

f) Various incentives were provided by the state to encourage labourers to enhance production.

4.3.2. Wages in the Private Sector

Scope of employment of slaves for production in the private sector was limited. The rules regarding slavery as laid down in Arthaśāstra (3/13) were:

i) Involuntary enslavement of a Aryan was punishable.

ii) Voluntary enslavement due to necessity was permissible only under certain special conditions.

iii) Only in case of the non-Aryans (mlechchas), they could be used as slaves.

iv) A slave used to enjoy various rights, e.g.

a) He could not be deprived of his wages and other privileges.

b) He could not be assigned to filthy work.

c) He used to enjoy the right to property and inheritance.

d) He could buy his freedom if willing and capable of doing so.

3/13/3-16: It is not an offence for Mlecchas to sell an offspring or keep it as a pledge.

4: But there shall be no slavery for an Arya in any circumstances whatsoever.

5: Or, after keeping as a pledge an Arya when the family has bound itself in times of distress of Aryas, they shall, on finding the redemption-amount, redeem first a minor or one who renders help.

6 A person pledging himself shall be forfeit if he runs away once, one pledged by another if (he runs away) twice, both at the first attempt, if about to leave for a foreign land.

7 Or, for one depriving a slave of his Aryahood, when he has stolen money, the fine shall be half (the above fines).

8 The pledger shall be liable for the capital, if the pledge has run away or is dead or is in calamity.

9 Making a pledge pick up a corpse, dung, urine or leavings of food, and making women (pledges) give bath to a naked person, giving corporal punishment to them and dishonouring them shall result in the loss of the capital, and shall result in freedom for a nurse, a female attendant, a woman tenant tilling for half the produce and a maid.

10 The going away of an attendant who has begotten an offspring is valid (in law).

11 For one approaching a nurse who is pledged, when she is unwilling, (the punishment shall be) the lowest fine for violence if she is under his control, the middle if she is under the control of another.

12 If one, himself or through another, defiles a maiden who is pledged, he shall lose the capital,

pay (her) dowry and a fine double that.

13 The progeny of one who sells himself shall be known as Arya.

14 He shall get what is earned by himself without detriment to his work for the master, also his paternal inheritance.

15 And he shall become an Arya by paying the price.

16 By that are explained the slave for livelihood and the person pledged.

Unlike many traditional economies, slave labour, in fact, used to play very little role in the private-sector production in the Arthaśāstra state. Labourers were to be employed by paying contractual wages. There is no indication that the state fixed private sector wages except in certain special cases. But the state put forward certain guidelines for determining wages in the private sector as would be clear from the following quotation:

"In the industries in private sector the state was keen to ensure that the labour was not exploited and the public was not cheated." (Altekar, 1962, p. 202)

The guidelines provided in different chapters of Arthaśāstra as regards wage determination in the private sector are:

1) Wages were to be settled by agreement between employees and employers. The following excerpts from Arthaśāstra corroborate this view:

i) 3/13/26: Those who are near shall note a labourer's engagement in work.

27: He should receive a wage as agreed upon, in conformity with the work and time (if the wage is not agreed upon).

28: A cultivator, a cowherd (and) a trader should receive one-tenth part of the crops, of butter (and) of the goods dealt in by them (respectively) if the wage is not agreed upon.

29: But if the wage is agreed upon, then as agreed upon.

ii) 3/14/19: Or, cultivators and traders shall give to a (partner) who has become ill in the interval between the commencement and completion of (work connected with) crops and goods (respectively) an individual share corresponding to work as done by him.

iii) 3/14/8: A wage is for work done, not for what is not done.

9: If after allowing even a little to be done, he does not allow it to be done (further), his work shall be considered as done.

10: In case the labourer misses the proper place and time or does the work in a wrong manner, he may not, if unwilling, allow the work as done.

11: In case more work is done than agreed upon, he shall not make the effort vain.

iv) 4/2/23: The Merchant should fix, after calculating their total earnings for the day, what the (sales-agents) should live on with permission.

2) It appears that the prevailing customs influenced wage agreements and wage determination in different localities. Sometimes experts' opinions were also sought in this regard, e.g.

3/13/30: But the group of those who work in hope (of remuneration) such as artisans, artists, minstrels, physicians, professional story-tellers, attendants and others should get a remuneration as others of that type do or as experts fix.

3) The wage agreement once settled were binding on both the parties and violation was subject to punishment as is evident in the following quotations from Arthaśāstra:

i) 3/13/33: In case of non-payment of the wage, the fine is one-tenth or six panas.

34: In case of denial, the fine is twelve panas or one-fifth.

ii) 3/14/1: For a labourer not doing the work after receiving the wage, the fine is twelve panas, and detention till it is done.

iii) 3/14/4: If, when there is a restriction 'You shall not give this work to another, nor shall I do anyone else's work,' the employer does not get work done by him or the labourer does not do the work, the fine shall be twelve panas.

iv) 4/1/2: Employers of artisans capable of making good an article, those good at entrusting materials, (and) artisans working with their own capital should accept entrusted material with the guarantee of the guild.

4: And they shall carry out the work with the place, time and (nature of the) work stipulated, without stipulation as to place or time if the nature of the work can be pointed out (as the reason).

5: For exceeding the time-limit, (there shall be) a reduction in the wage by one quarter and double that as fine.

6: They shall be liable for what is lost or destroyed except in case of deterioration or a sudden calamity.

7: For carrying out a work otherwise than as ordered, (there shall be) loss of wage and double that as fine.

4) The artisans in the Arthaśāstra state were organized under strong guilds with strong bargaining power and Kauṭilya considered that they were always ready to deceive the people or demand exorbitant charges from those who employed them.

4/1/65: In this manner the (king) should prevent thieves who are not known as thieves such as traders, artisans, actors, mendicants, jugglers and others from oppressing the country.

In order to prevent the artisans from exploiting common people, Arthaśāstra lays down several restrictive measures (4/1/..)

In the following cases, wage rates were also fixed by the state to ensure that exorbitant wages are not charged by artisans organized in strong guilds.

i) Making charges (for clothes):

4/1/10: The wage for weaving (shall be equal to) the value of the yarn, one and a, half times in the case of ksauma and kauseya, double in the case of patrorna, blankets and dukula.

ii) Washerman:

4/1/22 For the most precious (garments) the wage (shall be) one pana, for middling one half, for lowest one-quarter, for rough (garments) one masaka or two masakas, double for dyed (garments).

iii) Coins:

4/1/32: One masaka is the wage for one dharana of silver, one-eighth part (of a pane) for one suvarna (of gold).

33 In accordance with special skill, the wage may be increased to double.

iv) Articles of copper, steel, bell-metal, vaikrintaka and brass

4/1/35: In the case of copper, steel, bell-metal, vaikrntaka and brass, the wage is five (panas) per hundred (palas).

5) There were also measures for settlement of wage disputes in the following manner.

Disputes regarding work between the employer and the employee are to be settled only on the testimony of the witnesses. In the absence of witnesses the judge would conduct an inquiry at the place of work to arrive at a judgment pertaining to settlement of the dispute.

3/13/31: (Disputes) shall be settled only on the testimony of witnesses.

3/13/32: In the absence of witnesses, (the judge) should inquire at the place where the work (was carried out).

From the above discussion, the basic guidelines, as prescribed in Arthaśāstra as regards wage determination in the private sector, come out to be:

a) Wages were to be settled by agreements between the employers and the employees.

b) The wage agreements, once settled, were binding on both the parties and violation by any party was subject to punishment.

c) The artisans in the Arthaśāstra state were organized under strong guilds with considerable bargaining power. To prevent them from charging exorbitant wages, maximum fees and wages of artisans were fixed by the state in certain cases.

d) It was the duty of the state to ensure that private sector wages are so determined that the employer is not cheated and at the same time the labourer is not exploited.

4.4. Interest

Interest rates are to be rigidly fixed by the state (considering the degree of risk involved) so as to prevent usury and exploitation of the weak borrowers. Annual interest rates for various categories of borrowers are to be:

For non-commercial loans = 15%

For less risky commercial loans = 60%

For risky commercial loans = 120% and

For foreign trade = 240%.

If we closely look at the above chart, it is found that the rate of interest on loans for foreign trade (240% per annum) was much higher than that on loans for internal trade. This is quite contrary to the present day state policy pursued in India where, considering the chronic balance of payments crisis, it is desirable that interest on loans for foreign trade, esp. for exports, should be lower than that on loans for internal trade. The most feasible explanation for exorbitant rate of interest for foreign trade, as prescribed by Kauṭilya, lies in the very high risk involved in foreign trade in those days. During Kauṭilya's time, transport and communication systems were undeveloped. So, foreign trade was much more hazardous than internal trade. It is also noteworthy that modern commercial banks and lending institutions were non-existent in ancient time and most of the private money-lenders were not much resourceful. So, risk factor used to play a dominant role in determining the rate of interest. If we look closely at the chart for interest rates above, it is found that even in case of internal trade, interest rate increases according to the degree of risks involved in trading. Interest rate on loans for risky internal trade (120% per annum) is double of that on loans for hazard-free internal trade (60% per annum). By the same logic one may conclude that interest rate on loans for foreign trade, which involved much more risk (than internal trade), would be higher in general as compared to interest rates on loans for internal trade.

3/11/1: One paṇa and a quarter is the lawful rate of interest per month on one hundred paṇas, five paṇas for purposes of trade, ten paṇas for those going through forests, twenty paṇas for those going by sea.

3/11/2: For one charging or making another charge a rate beyond that, the punishment shall be the lowest fine for violence, for witnesses, each one of them, half the fine.

3/11/3: If, however, the king is unable to ensure protection, the (judge) should take into consideration the usual practice among creditors and the debtors.

3/11/4: Interest on grains (shall be) up to a half, on the harvesting crops; thereafter it may increase being turned into capital.

3/11/5: Interest on capital (shall amount to) half the profit, to be paid for one year, being set apart in a store.

4.5. Expenses for Transport, Storage and Maintenance of Security

The traders had to incur expenses for hiring caravans, travelling chariots, boats, ships and other conveyances. In many cases, traders travelling long distances had to pass through dense forests, deserts and other hazardous terrains. For crossing forests, they had to hire forest guards and for deserts, land pilots. Trade routes, in those days, were also infested with various extra-mundane hazards (ghosts, demons, etc. according to customary beliefs and legends). Merchants had to incur expenses (on priests, exorcists, etc. and for performing various rituals) to overcome these hazards. All the above expenses are to be taken into account while determining prices.

4.6. Tolls, Taxes and Surcharges

Commodity taxes as mentioned in Arthaśāstra may be divided into two major categories:

i) Taxes to be paid by the producers while selling commodities to traders who transported them to the specified market places for selling to the final users (as consumption goods or raw materials).

ii) Tolls to be paid at the entrance (toll-house) of major cities and towns.4

Arthaśāstra also mentions surcharges (vyaji):

2/16/10: One-sixteenth part is the surcharge in measure by capacity, one-twentieth part in measure by weighing, one-eleventh part of commodities sold by counting.

4.7. Profit

4.7.1. Profit in the Private Sector

a) Rate of profit in accordance with guidelines of Arthaśāstra is also to be rigidly fixed by the state so as to avoid uncertainty and to prevent traders from profiteering. There are also specific guidelines for ascertaining transport, storage and other associated expenses. Rigid and simplified rules are to be observed for determining tolls and taxes on all the commodities produced and traded. Higher profit rate is permissible for foreign trade. According to Arthaśāstra, the net profit for indigenous goods would be 5% and for foreign goods, 10%. Any trader, trying to earn a higher profit than prescribed by the state, would be punished with fines.

4/2/28: And he should fix a profit for them of five per hundred over and above the permitted purchase-price in the case of indigenous commodities, ten (per hundred) in the case of foreign goods.

b) Any trader, trying to earn a higher profit than prescribed by the state, would be punished with fines.

4/2/29: For those who increase the price beyond that or secure (a profit beyond that) during purchase or sale, the fine shall be two hundred paṇas for (an additional profit of) five paṇas in one hundred paṇas.

c) Higher rates were, however, permitted in case of certain imported commodities.

2/16/11: He should encourage the import of goods produced in foreign lands by (allowing) concessions.

2/16/12: And to those (who bring such goods) in ships or caravans, he should grant exemptions (from taxes) that would 'enable a profit (to be made by them).

4.7.2. Profit in the State Sector

The fixed rates of profit as prescribed in Arthaśāstra were meant for the private traders and manufacturers only. It appears that the state was in a position to charge higher rates of profit. Because of the advantage of employing labourers and artisans at wage rates lower than the rates prevailing in the private sector (due to stronger bargaining position of the state; facilities for employing subsistence and vishti labourers, etc.), the margin of profit earned by the state was likely to be higher than that of the private sector. The state could enhance prices (while the private producers and traders could not) in case of excess demand (2/16) and, thereby enjoy a higher margin of profit than the private traders and producers.

2/16/2: And that commodity which may be plentiful, he should collect in one place and raise the price.

2/16/3: Or, when the price is reached, he should fix another price.

2/16/4: He should establish in one place trade in royal commodities that are produced in his own country; in many places, in those produced in foreign lands.

The only restriction on the state was that:

2/16/6: And he should avoid even a big profit that would be injurious to the subjects.

From the above discussion on the basic guidelines for price determination in Arthaśāstra, it appears that the price policy in Arthaśāstra was well coordinated, coherent and uniform. There were also specific measures to be adopted for proper implementation of the price policy delineated in Arthaśāstra. They are discussed below.

4.8. Measures to Implement Price Policy

4.8.1. Administrative Measures

As regards implementation of price policy, a crucial role is to be played by the superintendent of the toll house (and officials of his department). Simultaneously with collection of tolls, he is entrusted with the task of implementing prices fixed by the superintendent of commerce.

2/21/1: The Collector of Customs and Tolls should establish the customs-house and the flag facing the east or the north in the vicinity of the big gates (of the city).

2/21/2: The receivers of duty, four or five in number, should record in writing (details about) traders who have arrived in a caravan, who they are, from what place, with how much merchandise and where the identity-pass (was issued) or the stamping was made.

If the concerned officials shirk their duties or adopt corrupt practices in connivance with the unscrupulous traders, they are to be punished.

14 The same (penalty) eightfold (shall be imposed) on the Superintendent concealing (the trader's offences).

It may be presumed that local administrators like the gopa and other officials of local administration used to maintain local prices. There is, however, no explicit mention of the officials responsible for the maintenance of local prices. But, from the tone of Arthaśāstra, it does not appear probable that private sellers or merchants were given a free hand in determining local prices or the invisible hand of demand and supply was permitted a free play in determining prices without state intervention.

4.8.2. Espionage Network

The espionage network is to play an important role in the implementation of price policy. False statements regarding costs and prices, adulteration, smuggling, overvaluation, under-valuation, etc. by the merchants, cannot be detected without the help of the spies.

Government officials, entrusted with the task of implementing price policy, would not resort to corrupt practices as they would always be alert that spies in different guises are looming large at every corner. Anybody, whatever be his apparent identity, may be a disguised spy and so, the fear of being detected and punished would automatically discourage merchants as well as government officials to resort to underhand practices by violating rules and procedures of price determination and price control laid down by the state.

i) 2/21/27: Or, a secret agent appearing as a trader should communicate to the king the size of the caravan.

2/21/28: In accordance with that information, the king should tell the Collector of Customs about the size of the caravan, in order to make his omniscience known.

2/21/29: Then the Collector, on meeting the caravan, should say, 'These are goods of high and low value belonging to such and such a merchant. It should not be concealed. This is the king's power.'

ii) 2/35/11: In the same manner, spies in the guise of traders should find out the quantity and price of the king's goods produced in his own country, obtained from mines, water-works, forests, factories and fields.

iii) 2/3512: And in activities concerning goods of high and low value produced in foreign lands (and) imported along a water-route or a land-route, they should find out the amount of duty, road cess, escort charges, dues at the police-station and the ferry, share, food and gifts.

iv) 2/35/13: In the same manner, agents.in the guise of ascetics, directed by the Administrator, should ascertain the honesty or dishonesty of farmers, cowherds and traders and of the departmental heads.

As regards the ubiquitous nature of the espionage network of Kauṭilya, a modern author opines: "There were spies in every traders' caravan." (Kosambi, D. D. 1981, P.147)

The espionage network is likely to facilitate perfect implementation of price policy by ensuring: (i) dissemination of correct information relevant to costs and prices, and (ii) prevention of corruption. (Mukherjee, Bharati 1976)

Accounting

Perfect accounting is an essential ingredient of successful implementation of any economic policy or programme. Here also, Arthaśāstra prescriptions claim admiration.

Detailed and accurate methods of accounting and auditing, as delineated in Arthaśāstra, reminds one of the accounting methods of a highly developed capitalist economy. Salaries of all the state employees should be paid promptly, all state orders ought to be in writing, power and duties of all the state departments should be clearly defined, separate registers are to be maintained for every item and accounts should be regularly entered in prescribed registers.

As regards the functions of the officers of different departments pertaining to auditing of the records of the respective departments, Kauṭilya prescribes detailed guidelines. All the officials related to these tasks are to be punctual and they should perform their duties honestly, diligently and with skill. Any dishonesty, negligence or lapses on their part would be punished with fines. In this regard Kauṭilya puts forward detailed guidelines resembling modern accounting practices.

The account books of different departments are to be presented in full before the audit officer in time. In case of delay due to unavoidable circumstances, some concessions in this regard may be made, but only up to a specified limit.

The guidelines for checking up of the accounts by the audit and accounts officer are also prescribed in detail by Kauṭilya. He mentions various restrictions on the accounts officer and punitive measures against him, in case he fails to discharge his assigned duties in a proper way.

According to Arthaśāstra prescriptions the director of stores should be conversant with receipts from outside and inside, for the current year and for many years before and after the current year, so that when asked he would not falter in respect of expenditure, balance and collections for these years. The accounts and finances of the different government departments are to be inspected regularly and with accuracy.

2/7/1: The Superintendent should cause the Record Office to be built facing the east or the north, with separate halls, (as) a place for record books.

2/7/2: There he should cause to be entered in the record-books: the extent of the number, activity and total (income) of the departments; the amount of increase or decrease in the use of the (various) materials, expenses, excess, surcharge, mixing, place, wages and labourers in connection with factories; the price, the quality, the weight, the measure, the height, the depth and the container in connection with jewels, articles of high value, of low value and forest produce; laws, transactions, customs and fixed rules of regions, villages, castes, families and corporations; the receipt of favours, lands, use, exemptions, and food and wages by those who serve the king; the receipt of jewels and land (and), the receipt of special allowances and (payments for) remedial measures against sudden calamities, by the king and his queens and sons; and payments and receipts in connection with peace and war with allies and enemies.

2/7/3: From that he should hand over in writing the (revenue) estimate, accrued revenue, outstanding revenue, income and expenditure, balance, (the time for) attendance (for audit), (sphere of) activity, customs and fixed rules, to all the departments.

2/7/16: The accounts should come in on Asadha full moon day.

2/7/17: When the (officers) have come with sealed account books and balances in sealed containers, he should impose restriction in one place, not allowing conversation (among them).

2/7/18: After hearing the totals of income, expenditure and balance, he should cause the balance to be taken away (to the treasury).

2/7/21: For (officers) not coming at the proper time or coming without the account-books and balances, the fine shall be one-tenth of the amount due.

2/7/22: And if, when the works officer presents himself, the accounts officer is not ready to audit, the lowest fine for violence (shall be imposed).

2/7/23: In the reverse case, the fine for the works officer (shall be) double.

2/7/24: The high officers should render accounts in full in accordance with their activity, without contradicting themselves.

2/7/25: And among these he who makes a divergent statement or speaks falsely shall pay the highest fine (for violence).

2/7/26: He should wait for one month, if the (officer) has not brought in the day-to-day accounts.

2/7/27: After the month, the (officer) shall pay a fine of two hundred paṇas increased (by that amount) for each succeeding month.

2/7/28: If an (officer) has a little of written balance due (from him), he should wait for five days.

2/7/29: If he brings in the day-to-day accounts after that period, preceded by (delivery of the balance into) the treasury, he should look into (the case) with reference to laws, transactions, customs and fixed rules and by totaling up, (and by looking at) the work actually carried out, by inference and the use of spies.

2/7/30: And he should check (the accounts) for each day, group of five days, fortnight, month, four months and year.

2/7/31: He should check the income with reference to the period, place, time, head of income, source, bringing forward, quantity, the payer, the person causing payment to be made, the recorder and the receiver.

2/7/32: He should check the expenditure with reference to the period, place, time, head (of expenditure), gain, occasion, the thing given, its use and amount, the person who orders, the person who takes out, the person who delivers and the receiver.

2/7/33: He should check the balance with reference to the period, place, time, head, bringing forward, the article, its characteristics, amount, the vessel in which it is deposited and the person guarding it.

2/7/34: If, in an affair of the king, the accounts officer is not ready for audit or disregards an order or changes the income and expenditure in a way different from the written order, the lowest fine for violence (shall be imposed).

2/7/35: For one writing down an item (in the accounts) without any order or in a wrong order or in an illegible manner, or twice over, the fine is twelve paṇas.

2/7/36: For one writing down the balance (in any of these ways) the fine is double (that).

2/7/39: In case of a false statement, the punishment is that for theft.

2/7/40: For admitted afterwards, (the fine is) double, so also if an item is forgotten and then brought in.

2/5/22: He should be conversant with receipts from outside and inside even after a hundred years, so that when asked he would not falter in respect of expenditure, balance and collections.

2/9/19: Therefore, he who is appointed by an order to a particular department shall communicate to him [i.e., the king] the real nature of that work and the income and expenditure (both) in detail and in the aggregate.

2/9/28: Therefore, his superintendents should carry out the works accompanied by accountants, writers, examiners of coins, receivers of balance and supervisors.

Buffer Stock

In Arthaśāstra much emphasis is laid on the maintenance of a buffer stocks of all commodities and replenishing them regularly so as to meet accidental shortages and thereby, to ensure smooth implementation of the price policy.

2/15/22: From these he should set apart one half for times of distress for the country people, (and) use the (other) half for times of distress for the country people, (and) use the (other) half.

2/15/23: And he should replace old (stock) with new.

4.9. Short Run and Long Run Aspects of Arthaśāstra Price Policy

The guidelines as scattered in various chapters of Arthaśāstra create the impression that there was a clear distinction between the short run and the long run aspects of price policy. Although the author did not use the modern terminologies, it is clear from the guidelines delineated in Arthaśāstra that the author well recognized the role of the forces of demand and supply. The short run and long run discrepancies between demand and supply were treated differently. Any sudden and short run excess demand and supply were not allowed to freely affect the pieces. The government endeavoured to stick to the existing prices and let the temporary discrepancy pass off. More important is that the private traders were never permitted to take advantage of temporary excess demand and generate a chaotic situation by creating artificial scarcities. At the same time, it was the duty of the government to see to it that traders do not incur losses as a consequence of temporary lack of demand.

It also appears from the observations in Arthaśāstra that the author was realistic enough to recognize that rigid prices could not be sustained under persistent discrepancies. So, if the discrepancies were found to be persistent, the government would have to revise the prices by pursuing a 'trial and error' method until the balance between demand and supply is restored. The government never attempted to artificially keep prices at a fixed level while long term demand and supply conditions did not permit so. There was no question of artificial 'floor price', 'ceiling price', etc. In case of persistent discrepancy between demand and supply, prices ought to be revised. But this adjustment was never left with the private traders. The superintendent of commerce was entrusted with the task of ascertaining, by 'trial and error', the exact degree of divergence between demand and supply and of readjusting prices accordingly.

4.9.1. Recognition of the Role of Demand and Supply

The following excerpt from Arthaśāstra corroborates the view that Kauṭilya could recognize the role of demand and supply in price determination.

2/16/1: The Director of Trade should be conversant with the differences in the prices of commodities of high value and of low value and the popularity or unpopularity of goods of various kinds, whether produced on land or in water (and) whether they have arrived along land-routes or water-routes, also (should 'know about) suitable times for resorting to dispersal or concentration, purchase or sale.

[Kauṭilya's equivalent for the modern term 'demand' is 'popularity of commodity', Chunder, 1995, p.139]

4.9.2. Temporary Discrepancy

It may be presumed that temporary excess demand (shortage of supply) was absorbed by releasing goods from the state storehouse which contained all the commodities transacted in the economy (2/15).

Although there is no specific mention that the commodities were released from the storehouse to take care of temporary excess demand, it may be inferred from the specific measures devised in Arthaśāstra to tackle temporary excess supply.

4/2/33: If there is a glut of commodities, the Director of Trade should sell all goods in one place.

4/2/34: So long as these are unsold, others shall not sell (those goods).

The above statement implies that if any commodity is in temporary excess supply, all private selling of the commodity would be prohibited so as to prevent downward movement of prices leading to confusion and losses to the sellers. The excess supply would be centralized by the state. Only this excess amount would be gradually released by the state according to existing demand. Once this excess amount is exhausted and demand-supply balance is restored, prohibition of sales of the commodity would be lifted. Here we see that, in case of excess supply, the gap is closed by the state by centrally storing the excess amount. By the same logic it may be presumed that in case of temporary excess demand the gap would be bridged by the state by resorting to opposite action, i.e. releasing commodities from the state storehouse.

All discrepancies between demand and supply are not, however, temporary phenomena. If the causes of discrepancy are deep seated, so that it appears to persist for a long time, the above mentioned measures would not bring about any lasting solution. The only way out in such a case is revision of prices. Kauṭilya recognized this fact and prescribed measures for price revision.

4.9.3. Persistent Discrepancy

The following excerpt from Arthaśāstra would through some light on the measures to tackle long term divergence between demand and supply:

2/16/2: And that commodity which may be plentiful, he should collect in one place and raise the price.

2/16/3: Or, when the price is reached, he should fix another price.

Two major conclusions may be drawn from the above statement. First, the state attached utmost importance to the commodities which were in wide use (in terms of both quantity transacted and types of use). The reason is clear. Prices of commodities, with insignificant use, are not likely to generate any serious problem. So, state intervention may not be necessary for such minor cases. But for major commodities with wide circulation and multiple use, irregularities in the price front may lead to serious consequences for the economy. So, state intervention is essential for such cases.

Secondly, the exact amount of price rise, necessary to restore balance, cannot be ascertained at the beginning. So Kauṭilya prescribes a step by step adjustment process:

2/16/2: And that commodity which may be plentiful, he should collect in one place and raise the price.

2/16/3: Or, when the price is reached, he should fix another price.

In case of excess supply, the state would collect the excess commodities and try to sell at the given price. If it is not possible to do so and if it becomes clear that the discrepancy is a long term one, the price would be revised downwards.

The above discussion makes it clear that Kauṭilya did never overlook the role of demand and supply in price determination and never attempted to keep prices at fixed levels while actual market forces did not permit so.

On the basis of the above principles regarding price determination as prescribed in Arthaśāstra we are to examine the nature of mathematical relationship involved in price determination and price revision in Arthaśāstra. It does not, however, mean that the mathematical exercises were actually done by the superintendent of commerce. It is more likely that 'trial and error' procedures were actually followed in this regard. That does not make it useless to look into the mathematical relationship that comes to the fore from the Arthaśāstra price mechanism.

So, in chapter-5, we are going to explain this formal relationship with the help of a simple arithmetic example with only six commodities, and the full-fledged mathematical model of price determination in the Arthaśāstra economy is presented in the Appendix to chapter-5 along with a hypothetical example with a large number of real commodities.

Chapter-5: Price Determination Model in Arthaśāstra

5.1. Introduction

In this chapter we are going to delineate the model of price determination as conceived in the Arthaśāstra of Kauṭilya. To start with we are to clarify why the model constructed here may be considered as a price determination model specifically meant for the Arthaśāstra economy and not simply a pure mathematical model roughly applicable to any (ancient or modern) economy. The basic premises of the model delineated here (rigid coefficient of production, rigid input proportions, categorization of products, specificity of various types of costs, the rules of exchange among various government departments, the peculiar government-trader-producer-consumer relation channel, the unidirectional input flows etc.) are peculiar to the Arthaśāstra economy (and to some extent to some other ancient Indian economies). But they do not have an iota of resemblance to any modern economy with sophisticated technologies, complicated production relations, control by the monopolies, no state control or badly managed state control etc. In fact, the model described here cannot be used to explain the way prices are actually determined in a modern economy. This does not, however, imply that this model has no relevance for any modern economy.

If the chaotic mechanism, of pricing in a modern economy (especially, the Indian Economy), be modified by competent authorities, Arthaśāstra model of price determination (modified according to the objective conditions of the modern age) would be a great help in bringing about order in price determination in a modern economy.

In the Arthaśāstra economy, the state used to play a pioneering role in the determination and regulation of the prices of goods and services produced in the country. This does not at all mean that the state used to fix the prices arbitrarily (whatever be the conditions of demand, supply and cost of production). On the contrary, the state used to regulate prices in such a way that cost of production is covered, producers and traders earn reasonable profit and at the same time no long term discrepancy between demand and supply could persist. In case of short term discrepancy, however, rigid prices were maintained till the discrepancy passed off. This was necessary to prevent the private traders from earning exorbitant profit by taking advantage of the crisis (in case of excess demand) leading to inconveniences of the buyers and, in case of excess supply, to save them from incurring losses by being compelled to sell at prices below costs. If, however, the discrepancy was persistent, the state used to take adequate steps to raise or reduce prices so as to remove long term discrepancy between demand and supply.

Form the study of Arthaśāstra, it appears that the state endeavoured to maintain fair prices that included costs of production and a reasonable margin of profit (5%) specified by the state,. This profit margin, however, was meant for the private sector only.

The producers' costs involved costs for raw materials, wages, interests on money invested in structures, implements and taxes. Traders' costs involved transport and associated costs, storage costs, taxes etc. For a given period of time, wages, interests, tolls & taxes, transport and storage costs etc. may be considered as given (by contracts, customs, state policies etc.) in the Arthaśāstra economy. These costs, taken together, would be denoted by 'other costs'. So, for a given private sector product, producers' sales price to the trader

= Raw material cost + other costs + 5% profit.

= 1.05 (raw material cost + other costs)

So, traders' sales price to the final users

= 1.05 (raw material cost + producers' other costs) + traders' other costs + traders' profit

= 1.05 {1.05(raw material cost + producers' other costs) + traders' other costs}

= 1.1 (raw material cost) + {1.1 (producers' other costs) + 1.05 (traders' other costs)}

On the other hand, state sector accounting prices

= 1.05 (raw material cost + other costs)

Now we proceed to explain the pricing method as described above with the help of a simple arithmetic example.

5.2. Arithmetic Example of Price Determination in the State Sector

Products Prices

Primary (agricultural) X_1 P_1

Primary (non-agricultural) X_2 P_2

Simple X_3, X_4 P_3, P_4

Advanced X_5, X_6 P_5, P_6

The state could charge a higher rate of profit (if necessary) while selling state sector commodities to the private sector.

For sake of simplicity we shall consider three types of prices in our discussion:

i) Inter-departmental sales prices of state sector commodities.

ii) Sales prices of state sector commodities to the private sector.

iii) Prices of commodities produced in the private sector.

In the state sector different commodities were produced under the guidance of the Directors or Superintendents of different departments. So, state sector products were to be circulated among different commodity producing departments (as inputs), for the state storehouse and for state sector consumption. All inter-departmental transactions were to be made in cash and with full account. Inter-departmental prices were determined by methods discussed below. For inter-departmental exchanges, we assume a profit rate of 5% (the standard rate prescribed in Arthaśāstra for private producers and traders). We also assume that the state used to sell some commodities, viz. non-agricultural primary products (for which the state used to enjoy absolute monopoly power over production) to the private traders. We may, however, relax this assumption and consider a more realistic case where the state used to sell to the private traders many other commodities, which were also produced in the private sector, but total private production was inadequate to meet total private sector demand. This relaxation of assumption would not qualitatively affect the essential features of the price determination model. In the first part of our study, however, we would stick to the assumption that the state sells only no-agricultural primary products (various metallic ores, oceanic products [conch shells, corals etc.] and forest products [plants, herbs, bones and hoofs of wild animals, etc.]) to the private sector.

The sales prices of these commodities to the private traders used to differ from inter-departmental prices by a higher profit margin. But this profit margin was not likely to be determined whimsically, nor was it altered frequently. From the nature of the Arthaśāstra state policies, it may be assumed that for a given period of time, this profit margin used to be rigidly determined by the state. The state sector products were sold to the private traders who transported them to the sales centres. So, sales prices of the traders to the final buyers (users of inputs or consumers) used to include transport and associated costs, tolls and taxes and permissible profit (5%).

Besides these non-agricultural primary products, all other commodities were produced in the private sector also. Prices of these products for the final users involved the following steps:

i) Producers' costs and profit, and

ii) Traders' costs and profit.

[For the state sector, products and prices are denoted by capital letters as already stated in chapter-3 of this study]

As in chapter-3, to distinguish different categories of products and their respective prices:

Agricultural products and their prices: bold-underlined letters

Non-agricultural primary products and their prices: italicized letters

Simple products: bold letters

Advanced products: simple Roman letters

Production coefficients (from chapter-3):

$\underline{\mathbf{a}}13 = 0.2$, $a24 = 0.3$, $\mathbf{a}34 = 0.3$, $\mathbf{a}35 = 0.1$, $\mathbf{a}36 = 0.2$, $\mathbf{a}43 = 0.5$, $\mathbf{a}45 = 0.2$, $\mathbf{a}46 = 0.4$, $a56 = 0.5$, $a65 = 0.4$.

Let the state sector prices of primary products be given as (pana per bhara)

$\underline{\mathbf{P}}1 = 5$ (agricultural) and $P2 = 10$ (non-agricultural)

Prices of State Sector Simple Products

To produce one unit of $\mathbf{X}3$, amount of $\underline{\mathbf{X}}1$ required is $\underline{\mathbf{a}}13 = 0.2$.

So, primary input cost for $\mathbf{X}3 = \underline{\mathbf{a}}13\underline{\mathbf{P}}1 = 0.2 \times 5 = 1.0$.

Again, to produce one unit of $X3$, amount of $X4$ required is $a43 = 0.5$.

So, simple input cost for $\mathbf{X}3 = \mathbf{a}43\ \mathbf{P}4 = 0.5\ \mathbf{P}4$

Let transport and other costs $= 1.0$.

So, total cost $= 1.0 + 0.5\ \mathbf{P}4 + 1.0 = 2 + 0.5\mathbf{P}4$

Therefore, price of $\mathbf{X}3$ including 5% profit

$\mathbf{P}3 = 1.05\ (2 + 0.5\ \mathbf{P}4) = 2.1 + 0.525\mathbf{P}4$ .... (1)

Similarly total cost of production for $\mathbf{X}4$

$=$ Primary input cost $+$ simple input cost $+$ transport and other costs

$= a24\ P2 + \mathbf{a}34\ \mathbf{P}3 + 2$ (given)

$= 0.3 \times 10 + 0.3\mathbf{P}3 + 2$

$= 5 + 0.3\ \mathbf{P}3$

So, price of $\mathbf{X}4$ (including 5% profit)

$\mathbf{P}4 = 1.05\ (5 + 0.3\ \mathbf{P}3) = 5.25 + 0.315\ \mathbf{P}3$ .... (2)

Solving equations (1) and (2) we get:

$\mathbf{P}3 = 5.82$ panas per bhara

$\mathbf{P}4 = 7.08$ panas per bhara

Prices of State Sector Advanced Products

Let transport and other costs for X5 and X6 are respectively 3 and 0.684.

So:

P_5 = 1.05 (simple input cost + advanced input cost + transport and other costs)

= 1.05 ($a_{35}P_3$ + $a_{45} P_4$ + $a_{65} P_6$ + 3)

= 1.05 (0.1x5.82 + 0.2x7.08 + 0.4 P_6 + 3)

= 5.2479 + 0.42 P_6 .... (3)

Similarly

P_6 = 1.05 (si9mple input cost + advanced input cost + transport and other costs)

= 1.05 ($a_{36} P_3$ + $a_{46} P_4$ + $a_{56} P_5$ + 0.684)

= 1.05 (0.2x5.82 + 0.4x7.08 + 0.5 P_5 + 0.684)

= 4.914 + 0.525 P_5 .... (4)

Solving equations (3) and (4) we get:

P_5 = 9.38 panas per bhara

P_6 = 9.84 panas per bhara

5.3. Private Sector

Price of x_1 (agricultural product) is higher in the private sector than in the state sector because of higher production cost. Let private sector's user price of x_1 (including transport and other costs, and producer's and trader's profits):

p_1 = 10 panas per bhara.

Now, state sector sales price of x_2

= State sector accounting price of x_2 + 10% profit

= 1.01x10 = 10.1 panas per bhara.

Let transport and other costs = 1.9

So, with 5% trader's profit:

p_2 = 1.05 (10.1 + 1.9) = 1.05x12 = 12.6 panas per bhara.

Prices of Simple Products

Let transport and other costs for x_3 and x_4 are respectively 1 and 1 for the producers and 3 and 5 for the traders.

Producer's cost for x_3 = primary input cost + simple input cost + transport and other costs

$= a_{13}p_1 + a_{43}p_4 + 1 = 0.2 \times 10 + 0.5p_4 + 1 = 3 + 0.5p_4$

So producer's sales price to traders (including 5% producer's profit)

$= 1.05 (3 + 0.5p_4) = 3.15 + 0.525p_4$

Trader's cost for x_3 = $3.15 + 0.525p_4$ + trader's transport and other costs

$= 3.15 + 0.525p_4 + 3.0 = 6.15 + 0.525p_4$

So final user's price (including 5% trader's profit)

$= 1.05 (6.15 + 0.525p_4) = 6.4575 + 0.55p_4$ .... (5)

Now, producer's cost for x_4 = primary input cost + simple input cost + transport and other costs

$= a_{24}p_2 + a_{34}p_3 + 1 = 0.3 \times 12.6 + 0.3p_3 + 1 = 4.78 + 0.3p_3$

So producer's sales price to traders (including 5% producer's profit)

$= 1.05 (4.78 + 0.3p_3) = 5.019 + 0.315p_3$

Trader's cost for x_4 = $5.019 + 0.315p_3 + 5$ (trader's transport and other costs) $= 10.019 + 0.315p_3$

So final user's price (including 5% trader's profit)

$= 1.05 (10.019 + 0.315p_3) = 10.52 + 0.33p_3$ .... (6)

Solving equations (5) and (6) we get

$p_3 = 14.96$ panas/bhara

$p_4 = 15.46$ panas/bhara

Relevant state sector prices (as calculated earlier)

$P_3 = 5.82$ panas/bhara

$P_4 = 7.08$ panas/bhara

Prices of Advanced Products

Let transport and other costs for x_5 and x_6 are respectively 3 and 1.9 for the producers and 5 and 1.86 for the traders.

Producer's cost for x5 = simple input cost + advanced input cost + transport and other costs

$$= a_{35}p_3 + a_{45}p_4 + a_{65}p_6 + 3$$

$$= 0.1 \times 14.96 + 0.2 \times 15.46 + 0.4p_6 + 3$$

$$= 7.588 + 0.4p_6$$

So, producer's sales price to traders (including 5% producer's profit)

$$= 1.05 \,(7.588 + 0.4p_6)$$

$$= 7.967 + 0.42p_6$$

Trader's cost for x5

$$= 7.967 + 0.42p_6 + 5$$

$$= 12.967 + 0.42p_6$$

So including 5% trader's profit:

$$p_5 = 1.05 \,(12.967 + 0.42p_6)$$

$$= 13.615 + 0.441p_6 \quad\text{————————————————————(7)}$$

Producer's cost for x6 = simple input cost + advanced input cost + transport and other costs

$$= a_{36}p_3 + a_{46}p_4 + a_{56}p_5 + 2$$

$$= 0.2 \times 14.96 + 0.4 \times 15.46 + 0.5p_5 + 1.9$$

$$= 11.076 + 0.5p_5$$

So, producer's sales price to traders (including 5% producer's profit)

$$= 1.05 \,(11.076 + 0.5p_5)$$

$$= 11.63 + 0.525p_5$$

Trader's cost for x6

$$= 11.63 + 0.525p_5 + 1.86$$

$$= 13.49 + 0.525p_5$$

So including 5% trader's profit:

$$p_6 = 1.05 \,(13.49 + 0.525p_5)$$

$$= \qquad\qquad 14.165 \qquad\qquad +$$

$0.551\rho 5$———————————————————————(8)

Solving equations (7) and (8) we get:

$\rho 5$ = 26.24 panas/bhara.

$\rho 6$ = 28.62 panas/bhara.

Relevant state sector prices:

P5 = 9.38 panas/bhara.

P6 = 9.84 panas/bhara.

Thus we see that private sector prices are much higher than state sector accounting prices.

The matter, however becomes complicated if we introduce a large number of commodities and large number of interdependent relations as in the real Arthaśāstra economy. This complicated situation could, however, be handled with a suitable mathematical model, which is given in the Appendix.

It may be presumed that these complicated matters in the real Arthaśāstra economy had been settled by long historical process and by 'trial and error'.

In the above example, while considering the sales prices for the final users, we have assumed constant transport cost for each product. This implies that a product is carried to the same distance and passes through the same number of tollhouses to reach the final destination. This may not be so in reality. Moreover, if a product is produced in different localities, wages and associated costs may differ because of differences in local customs and practices. Thus the sales prices, offered by traders coming from different localities, may differ. In such a situation, under free-market mechanism, the lowest prices are likely to prevail, or, demand conditions may determine the market prices. Traders who cannot afford to sell at the market-determined price would be competed out. [Here the term 'free-market mechanism', in the context of an economy with full state-control, may appear anomalous. But we have discussed in earlier chapters that state-control in the Arthaśāstra economy was radically different from that in a so called socialist economy, mixed economy or any variant of authoritarian economy of the modern world. State-control in the Arthaśāstra economy was to ensure the free play of the market forces by preventing monopoly traders from generating market imperfections or creating crisis by taking advantage of shortages.]

The static equilibrium situation as described above will be achieved by trial-and-error process. In our static model we have assumed that such a situation has already been achieved in each selling centre, i.e. a given price of a commodity prevails, being approved by the state, in each market. No experienced trader would approach a market where the prevailing price is less than his offer price. In case of unanticipated rise in market clearing price due to sudden rise in demand, the state would appropriate the additional gain due to price rise. On the other hand, in case of unanticipated fall in market price, the state would compensate the businessman.

One important aspect (which has some resemblance with the product differentiation in a modern economy) of the Arthaśāstra economy is worth mentioning here. In those days, similar craft products produced in different localities differed considerably from each other in terms of quality, technological specifications or at times, psychological appeal to the buyers of the name of the place associated with the product. Each locality had developed its methods by historical evolution, heredity and by the caste system. Unlike in modern days, globalization of technology was not possible in those days. Technological secrets were well guarded. Specialized skills could not be imitated unless taught directly by the expert. So, the users treated these products of different localities, although apparently similar, as different commodities. In Arthaśāstra, similar products, produced at different localities have been mentioned with the names of the respective localities tagged with the product name, e.g.

Blankets made at Kāśī = Kāśika

Cotton Fabrics made at Kalinga = Kalingaka

Fibrous Garments made at Magadha = Māgadhikā

In the Arthaśāstra state, each local authority used to know the price (as determined in the above manner) of each commodity exchanged in the locality. They were to see to it that private traders and producers do not charge prices different from ones justifiable by the basic principles of price determination. For goods entering Into a locality (with the traders), the earlier government-seals indicated the place of origin, distance travelled, journey-routes etc. Spies also used to provide necessary information in this regard. So, it was quite easy for the local authorities to ascertain the justifiable sales-price of a commodity brought by the traders from another place and brought to the locality under consideration. The traders were not likely to make false statements with a view to making higher profit as, in that case, they could be easily detected (spies were lurking in every corner) and punished.

It is quite unlikely that any mathematical model as elaborated in this study [in the appendix to this chapter] were used to determine the prices. Most probably, prices were determined by trial-and-error process. Whatever be the actual process, it appears from the spirit of Arthaśāstra that prices determined by the Arthaśāstra state were god approximations to the prices that could be determined by our mathematical model, or for that matter, any coherent and consistent method. So, it was not necessary that the Superintendent of Commerce and his officials had to be well versed in mathematical tools to handle stylized models. In a simple economy like the Arthaśāstra economy, basic arithmetic common sense and power to observe objective forces properly were sufficient to have a good grasp of the method of determining prices in reality. Information provided by the spies was of considerable help in this regard.

So, considering the limited number of commodities, small population, limited number of toll-houses and selling-centres, simple and rigid technology, administrative efficiency of the state and perfect information mechanism through the spies, it is not unrealistic to presume that prices determined or approved by the authorities in the Arthaśāstra state closely approximated the prices that could be determined theoretically by the mathematical models [as delineated in Appendix to this chapter].

So far, we have assumed that the state used to sell only the non-agricultural primary products to the private traders. If we relax this assumption and consider the possibility of the state selling all sorts of commodities to the private sector, our pricing model, as expounded so far, will have to be modified slightly without altering the basic principles. The matter is discussed in detail in the next section.

5.4. Extended Pricing Model

In this section, we assume that many commodities produced in the private sector are inadequate to meet the consumption and input requirements of this sector. So9, the gap is filled by state sector sales of these products to the private sector. In such a case, state sector sales price would serve as a guideline for pricing in the private sector as in the case of non-agricultural primary products. According to the principle:

User's price = State sector accounting price + state sector additional profit + trader's transport and other costs + tolls and taxes paid by the traders + 5% profit of the traders.

For the jth product (primary, simple, advanced):

$\rho_j = \{(1 + \pi_j)P_j + \sigma_j\} + $ trader's profit $= 1.05\{(1 + \pi_j)P_j + \sigma_j\}$

Where, π_j = rate of state sector additional profit for the jth product.

σ_j = traders' transport and associated costs + tolls and taxes for the jth product.

In this case, the state would adjust π_j in such a way that user's price will be the same for both the state sector and the private sector producers.

The case of state sector sales to private sector as discussed is explained diagrammatically in diagram 5.2. In 5.2a, the market-determined price (which is higher than the users' price determined on the basis of state sector sales price) appears too high by the standards of the state. Now, the state fixes the users' price at p_1 to force out the high cost traders and producers. At this price excess demand is q_1q_2, which is covered by state sector sales. In 5.2b, private sector supply (q^*) is too inadequate to meet private sector requirements (q) at the reasonable price (p). So, the state sells q^*q amount of the commodity to the private sector.

So far, we have considered the static price-determined model where a static equilibrium situation has been arrived at by trial-and-error. A highly relevant question, however, is how any change in demand, production coefficients and state policy or any sudden change (brought about by war, natural calamities etc.) could be incorporated in the above model. This brings us to the dynamic aspects of the model to be discussed in the following section.

5.5. Dynamic Aspects of Price Determination

So far, we have considered a situation where, under certain given conditions, different commodities are produced in the state sector and the private sector. Each commodity has a user's price. The Superintendent of Commerce, with the help of local officials and the espionage network, maintains these prices. These prices lead to a balance between demand and supply in the market for each commodity. Now, we are going to examine (in the following subsection) the state's reaction to discrepancies (temporary or persistent) between demand ans supply generated by extraneous forces.

5.5.1. Temporary Discrepancy

Let there be excess demand for some commodities and excess supply of some other commodities. Excess demand may arise due to increase in population, increase in production of goods using the product under consideration as input, establishment of new villages and towns, construction of roads, increase in demand of the rich, production-failure due to natural calamities, wars etc. Excess supply, on the other hand, may arise due to fall in demand, over-production etc.

According to Arthaśāstra principles, under these circumstances, the private traders or producers were not permitted to alter the existing prices without the approval of the state. The Department of Commerce alone had the power to revise the prices. If it appeared certain that the causes for excess demand or excess supply were purely transitory and they would soon pass off restoring the normal conditions, the Superintendent of Commerce would not revise the existing prices. In case of excess demand, the state may release relevant commodities from the buffer stock or simply force the users to restrict demand temporarily. In case of excess supply, on the other hand, the state would restrict sales and production of commodities in excess supply until the normal situation returns.

To quote from Arthaśāstra: (4.2.33-35):

33 If there is a glut of commodities, the Director of Trade should sell all goods in one place.

34. So long as these are unsold, others shall not sell (those goods).

35 The (agents) shall sell those for a daily wage for the benefit of the subjects.

5.5.2. Persistent Discrepancy

If any discrepancy between demand and supply persisted and did not appear to pass away, the Department of Commerce would have to announce revised prices itself or approve (after verification by the officials on the basis of the reports of the spies) the revised prices put forward by traders and producers. Let us consider the case of excess demand. In such a situation, even if the commodities were produced exclusively in the private sector, private traders or producers were not permitted to determine the revised prices unless approved by the state officials. The private traders or producers might announce the revised prices to the state officials who would then verify whether the revisions were done according to Arthaśāstra principles. If the announced prices were correct, they would be approved. In case of wrong announcements out of ignorance, the prices would be corrected. But in case of deliberate wrong announcements (to be detected by spies in various guises), the alleged trader or producer would be punished.

Generally, price revision, in case of persistent discrepancy, was done stage by stage and by trial-and-error process.

To quote from Arthaśāstra (2.16.2-3):

2 And that commodity which may be plentiful, he should collect in one place and raise the price.

3 Or, when the price is reached, he should fix another price.

If the relevant commodities were purely final consumption goods, these price increases would not have any repercussions on the prices of other commodities. In this case, the state would go on increasing prices itself (or go on insisting the traders and the producers to announce enhanced prices to be approved by the state) until the balance between demand and supply is restored for the relevant final consumption goods.

If, however, the relevant goods were used as inputs for other products, initial price increase would affect cost of production and prices of all products that used as inputs, directly or indirectly, the goods the prices of which had been increased. Each stage of price increase of the commodities with excess demand would have to be accompanied by revision of prices of many other commodities also. This process is discussed in the next subsection with the help of an arithmetic example.

5.5.3. Extraneous Increase in Sales Price of State Sector Commodities

Let the state sector increase additional rate of profit on X_2 (for sales to private traders) from 10% to 100%.

Now state sector sales price of x_2

= State sector accounting price of x_2 + 100% profit

= 10 + 100% of 10 = 20 panas/bhara.

With trader's transport and other costs of 1.9 and 5% trader's profit:

$p_2 = 1.05 (20 + 1.9) = 1.05 \times 21.9 = 23$ [approx.] panas/bhara.

$p_1 = 10$ panas/bhara [same as before]

Prices of Simple Products

We have already stated that transport and other costs for **x3** and **x4** are respectively 1 and 1 for the producers and 3 and 5 for the traders.

x3 does not require x_2 as input

So, user's price for **x3**:

$p_3 = 6.4575 + 0.55p_4$ .... (9) [unchanged]

Now, producer's cost for **x4** = primary input cost + simple input cost + transport and other costs

$= a_{24}p_2 + a_{34}p_3 + 1 = 0.3 \times 23 + 0.3p_3 + 1 = 7.9 + 0.3p_3$

So, producer's sales price to traders (including 5% producer's profit)

$= 1.05 (7.9 + 0.3p_3) = 8.295 + 0.315p_3$

Trader's cost for x4:

$= 8.295 + 0.315p_3 + 5$ (trader's transport and other costs)

$= 13.295 + 0.315p_3$

So, user's price (including 5% trader's profit):

$p_4 = 1.05 (13.295 + 0.315p_3) = 13.96 + 0.33p_3$ .... (10)

Solving equations (9) and (10) we get

$p_3 = 17.27$ panas/bhara

$p_4 = 19.66$ panas/bhara

Thus we see that although **x3** does not use x_2 as input, its price has been affected by the change in p_2 because of indirect effect through the change in p_4.

Prices of Advanced Products

We have already stated that transport and other costs for x5 and x6 are respectively 3 and 1.9 for the producers and 5 and 1.86 for the traders.

Producer's cost for x_5

= simple input cost + advanced input cost + transport and other costs

$$= a_{35}p_3 + a_{45}p_4 + a_{65}p_6 + 3$$

$$= 0.1 \times 17.27 + 0.2 \times 19.66 + 0.4p_6 + 3$$

$$= 8.695 + 0.4p_6$$

S0, producer's sales price to traders (including 5% producer's profit)

$$= 1.05 \, (8.695 + 0.4p_6)$$

$$= 9.09 + 0.42p_6$$

Trader's cost for x_5

$$= 9.09 + 0.42p_6 + 5$$

$$= 14.09 + 0.42p_6$$

So (including 5% trader's profit)

$$p_5 = 1.05 \, (14.09 + 0.42p_6)$$

$$= 14.79 + 0.441p_6 \text{————————————————(11)}$$

Producer's cost for x_6

= simple input cost + advanced input cost + transport and other costs

$$= a_{36}p_3 + a_{46}p_4 + a_{56}p_5 + 1.9$$

$$= 0.2 \times 17.27 + 0.4 \times 19.66 + 0.5p_5 + 1.9$$

$$= 13.218 + 0.5p_5$$

S0, producer's sales price to traders (including 5% producer's profit)

$$= 1.05 \, (13.218 + 0.5p_5)$$

$$= 13.88 + 0.525p_5$$

Trader's cost for x_6

$$= 13.88 + 0.525p_5 + 1.86$$

$$= 15.74 + 0.525p_5$$

So (including 5% trader's profit)

$$P_6 = 1.05 \, (15.74 + 0.525p_5)$$

$= 16.53 + 0.551\ p_5$————————————————-(12)

Solving equations (11) and (12) we get

$P_5 = 29.15$ panas/bhara

$P_6 = 32.56$ panas/bhara

COMPARISON OF PRICES

ORIGINAL PRICE REVISED PRICE

(panas/bhara)   (panas/bhara)

	ORIGINAL PRICE (panas/bhara)	REVISED PRICE (panas/bhara)
p_1	10	10
p_2	12.6	23
p_3	14.96	17.27
p_4	15.46	19.66
p_5	26.24	29.15
p_6	28.62	32.56

Chapter-6: Arthaśāstra and Price Policy in India during the Plan Period

6.1: In this chapter we are going to look into the salient features of the price policy adopted in India during the plan period and point out its similarities and dissimilarities with the price policy in Arthaśāstra as discussed in the preceding chapters.

Notwithstanding the radical differences between the democratic political system of present day India and the centralized monarchy as conceived in Arthaśāstra, the price control mechanism in the two systems has some common features worth making a comparative study.

Under the mixed economic planning in India, prices are not left completely to the free play of market forces. For all the commodities produced in the state sector and many commodities produced in the private sector, prices are administered by the state. This has given rise to a system of dual prices – administered prices along with prices determined by the market forces. The basic features of the price mechanism, as pursued in India during the plan period, are discussed in section 6.2. In section 6.3., the price control mechanism in modern India is compared with that in Arthaśāstra.

6.2. Price Policy during the Plan Period in India

Basic Objectives

The basic objectives of the price policy in India during the plan period in India are the following (Jha, 1968):

1. To protect the interests of the vulnerable sections of the population.

2. To guide investment to desired channels.

3. To prevent hoarders from increasing prices by taking advantage of shortages.

In spelling out the basic objectives of the price policy to be pursued in India, L. K. Jha, the then Governor of the Reserve Bank of India pointed out (Jha, 1968, pp. 478-480) that prices in an LDC like India could by no means be left to be determined by market forces, where, instead of free competition, monopolistic control prevails. Food prices are to be stabilized as they lead to all round price increase. Savings gap and foreign exchange deficit are two other causes requiring price control. In an LDC like India, there is the need for building up a wide range of facilities where commercial considerations of maximum direct return on investments do not or cannot always apply.

In brief, the basic objectives of the Price Policy as pursued in India during the Plan Period boil down to:

i) Ensuring availability of essential commodities at moderate prices to the weaker sections of the population.

ii) Encouraging production by providing price incentives to the producers in the private sector.

iii) To channel resources to the desired directions so that targets of the Plans are fulfilled.

The consequences of the endeavour by the government to achieve these objectives are stated below.

i) Administered Prices of various agricultural and industrial products.

ii) Public Distribution of food grains and many other essential goods.

iii) Huge subsidies arising out of the twin contradictory objectives of providing price incentives to the producers and provision of low-priced essential goods to the consumers [Economic Survey, Govt. of India, Various issues].

These features are discussed in detail in the following subsection.

Administered Prices of Industrial Products

Prices of a large number of industrial raw materials and intermediaries like Iron & Steel, Coal, Cement, Aluminium, Petroleum Products, Drugs, Fertilizers, etc. and of Electricity are fixed by the government. The Bureau of Industrial Costs and Prices (BICP) are entrusted with the task of determining the prices of these commodities. Generally, the 'Cost-Plus' method is adopted in this case. The Seventh and the Eighth Plans, various issues of Report on Currency and Finance (RBI) and Economic Survey (Govt. of India) reveal the following disquieting features of the administered pricing of industrial products in India:

i) No uniform rule is applied to determine the prices of industrial products. Price is fixed separately for each product on the basis of various criteria like cost, capacity utilization, standard of efficiency, etc. Diversity of producers leads to confusion and inefficiency.

ii) Production costs are determined by the BICP on the basis of inadequate and backdated data.

iii) In many cases, inefficiencies are encouraged and cost reducing innovations discouraged as inefficiencies could be covered by administered price-hikes.

iv) Having no firm basis of determining cost and change in it, there are frequent price changes and, at times, prices of all the important intermediaries are raised simultaneously. This leads to widespread price rise.

In fact, instead of having control over the prices, the Price-Controlling Authorities are themselves being controlled by unpredictable extraneous forces, which force them to raise Administered Prices at inappropriate times, even if this may have highly adverse impact on the economy of the country. Various facts point out that one of the major causes of inflation in India has been the rise in Administered Prices (The Hindu Survey of Indian Industry, 1996, p.15).

It is sometimes held that the major cause of inflation in India, since the Second Five Year Plan, has been the huge amount of deficit financing and the consequent rapid increase in money supply. But analytical studies have revealed that, in India, increase in money supply and price-hike are not very strongly correlated.

V. Pandit (1993, p.40) points out:

"There are, however, good reason to believe that this relationship is not as strong as often believed to be, though diametrically opposite view that money supply exerts no pressure on prices is not sustainable, the growing recognition that cost factors play a vital role in determining the course of price movement is supported on empirical as well as analytical grounds."

The following table shows the relation between monetary growth and overall price rise in India.

Table-1: Money Supply and Price Rise in India

Year	Growth of M-1 (%)	Growth of M-3 (%)	Rate of Overall Price Rise (%)
1983-84	15.9	17.9	7.5
1984-85	19.9	18.7	6.5
1885-86	10.0	16.1	4.4
1986-87	17.4	18.8	5.8
1987-88	12.7	15.3	8.2
1988-89	15.5	18.4	7.5
1989-90	21.7	20.2	7.4
1990-91	14.4	14.9	10.3
1991-92	18.1	18.5	13.7

Source: V. Pandit, 1993, p.40
[According to Reserve Bank of India (RBI)

M-1 = Coins and Currency Notes with the public + Demand Deposits in commercial banks + other deposits with the RBI.

M-3 = M-1 + Time Deposits in commercial banks.]

From Table-1, the Correlation Co-efficient between M-1 and price-rise, and M-3 and price-rise are found respectively as $r_{1P} = 0.22$ and $r_{3P} = -0.06$

Thus it is seen that the view, that increase in money supply is the most important cause of inflation in India, is hardly supported by statistical evidence. On the other hand, the increase in Administered Prices is a very significant cause of inflation in India. The rate of increase in the prices of Administered Industrial Products (weight = 15.929), comprising mainly energy inputs, viz. Petroleum, Electricity, Coal and Urea, is shown in the following table.

Table-2: Price Rise of Administered Industrial Products

Year	Rise in Prices of Administered Industrial Products as a Group (%)
1984-85	17.50
1985-86	28.03
1986-87	14.42
1987-88	17.53
1988-89	22.83
1989-90	19.00
1990-91 to 1994-95 (Average Annual)	11.30
1995-96	01.70
1996-97	11.00
1999-2000	15.10
2000-2001	28.10

Source: Economic Survey, Govt. of India, 1984-85 to 2000-2001

Table-2 shows that, except for the year 1995-96, the rise in Administered Prices of some major industrial products (intermediate and basic products) had been considerable. This had widespread effects on the price front, as these products are essential inputs for a large number of industrial products. The group, considered above, does not include administered items like Cement, Aluminium, Iron and other Metallic products, Drugs, Sugar, etc. The overall contribution of administered items to inflation in 1999-2000 and 2000-2001 were respectively 64.6 percent and 62.8 percent.

In many cases, there is Dual Pricing, i.e. Administered Prices coexist with Market-determined Prices. The Dual Pricing Policy was first adopted for the price of Steel. Later on, it was extended to many other essential industrial products like Sugar, Edible Oils, Cement and cheaper varieties of Cotton Cloth. In many cases (e.g. Sugar), Dual Pricing resulted in abnormal price-rise in the open market. Sometimes, rise in Administered Prices gives signal to the businessmen to raise prices in the open market.

Subsidies for Industrial Products

Maintenance of Administered Prices, in general, compels the government to subsidize administered items, which generates heavy pressure on the exchequer. Very often, sudden withdrawal of subsidies, in order to reduce Fiscal Deficits, creates serious problems for the economy, which could have been avoided had the prices been permitted to be determined by market forces from the very beginning. The most serious adverse impact is generated by increase in prices of Petroleum Products as a consequence of withdrawal of subsidies (The Hindu Survey of Indian Industry, 1996, p.187).

Agricultural Prices

The tween objectives of Agricultural Price Policy in India are:

a) To encourage producers of crops to increase production by assured and remunerative prices.

b) To provide essential food articles to the poor consumers at reasonable prices.

[RBI: Report on Currency and Finance, 1986-87, Vol.-I, p.122]

To achieve the first of these objectives, Minimum Support Prices (MSP) and Procurement Prices of agricultural products are announced by the government every year. To fulfill the second objective, Public Distribution System has been adopted. MSPs are formulated each year by the recommendations of the Commission for Agricultural Costs and Prices (CACP). These recommendations are based on a detailed study of costs of production and other relevant facts. The major crops for which CACP recommends MSPs are – Paddy, Wheat, Jowar, Bajra, Maize, Ragi, and Barley; Pulses – Gram, Arhar, Moong, and Urad; Oilseeds – Groundnut, Sunflower, Rapeseed, Mustard, Safflower, Toria and Copra; and Commercial Crops – Soya been, Cotton, Jute, Sugarcane and Tobacco.

Procurement Prices announced by the government are based on the MSPs recommended by the CACP, the government's perception of the replenishment needs for food stocks, and free market price behaviour (Economic Survey, 1994-95, pp.80-82).

Procurement Prices and MSPs of some important agricultural commodities are given in the following table.

Table-3: Minimum Support Price (M)/Procurement Price (P) for Crops (Rs./Quintal)

CROPS	PRICE TYPE	1990-91	2000-2001	PERCENTAGE INCREASE
PADDY (Common)				
WHEAT				
GRAM				
COTTON				
GROUNDNUT				
JUTE				
RAPESEED/ MUSTARD				
SOYABEEN				

Source: Economic Survey, Govt. of India, 2000-2001, Table-5.5, p. S-68

The actual operation of the policy relating to the MSPs and Procurement Prices has produced the following outcomes which are hardly in conformity with the desired objectives:

i) Most of the beneficiaries of the MSPs and Procurement Prices are the big farmers and landlords. The vast majority of the small cultivators are compelled, at harvest times, to sell their crops to the traders and money lenders, who appropriate all the gains from continuously rising MSPs and Procurement Prices.

ii) The data-base, on which CACP determines agricultural costs are inadequate and backdated, and the decisions to upgrade MSPs do not spring from any objective reason, but, in most of the cases, out of the pressure from the powerful lobbies with vested interests, who pay little heed to the interest of the country.

According to Economic Survey (1994-95, p.77), two major causes of inflation in India are:

a) Spillover effects of administered price-increase in Wheat, Rice, Sugar and Energy Products.

b) Cumulative impact of continuously increasing MSPs.

Table-3 shows that there has been continuous rise in the MSPs and Procurement Prices of the major agricultural commodities during the last decade. One of the effects of this trend is continuous 'cost-push' rise in prices of industrial products using agricultural raw materials like jute, cotton, etc. The impact of rise in prices of food grains has been most serious.

The Report of the Expenditure Reform Commission suggested phasing out of 'producer's subsidy' by moderating the increase in MSPs. But the main obstacle on the path of i8mplementation of this recommendation is the Vested Interest Lobby (big farmers, landlords, and owners of modern agricultural farms), which has considerable control over the "Vote-Bank' that decides the fate of the decision making Politicians and Political Parties.

Public Distribution System (PDS) in India

One of the major objectives of the Agricultural Price Policy in India, during the Plan Period, was to assure steady supply of essential food grains to the consumers, especially, the poor and the middle class, at affordable prices. To quote:

"The objective of the Government's food security policy is to ensure availability of food grains to the public at affordable prices. The Public Distribution System, which has existed in the country since the Second World War, strives to meet these twin objectives" Economic Survey, Govt. of India, 1994-95, p.80).

Wheat and Rice, the two principal cereal food crops in India, are issued by the Central Government at uniform Central Issue Prices (CIPs) to states and union territories for distribution under PDS. The Food Corporation of India (FCI), a government agency, procures and issues the crops to the states and the union territories. The 'Economic Cost' of the FCI involves costs for procurement, storage, distribution, and wastage of food grains. The gap, between FCI's 'Economic Cost' and realization based on the Central Issue Prices, is filled by the Central Government through 'Food Subsidy'.

With the adoption of the 'New Economic Policy' since 1991, the necessity to reduce Fiscal and Revenue Deficits called for reduction of all sorts of subsidies. To this end, the Central Issue Prices of the two major cereals, viz. Rice and Wheat have been revised upwards several times since 1990-91 as shown in the following table.

Table-4: Periodic Revision of Central Issue Prices of Wheat and Rice (Rs./Quintal)

	WHEAT		RICE	
	Price	% Change	Price	% Change
1990-91	234	—————	289	—————
1991-92	280	19.7	377	30.4
1992-93	280	0.0	377	0.0
1993-94	330	17.9	437	15.9
1994-95	402	21.8	537	22.9
1995-96	402	0.0	537	0.0
1996-97	402	0.0	537	0.0
1997-98: BPL	250	—————	350	—————
APL	450	—————	700	—————
1998-99: BPL	250	0.0	350	0.0
APL	650	44.4	905	29.3
1999-2000: BPL	250	0.0	350	0.0
APL	682	4.9	905	0.0
2000-2001: BPL	415	66.0	565	61.4
APL	830	21.7	1130	24.9

Source: Economic Survey, 2000-2001, Table-5.11, p.95.

BPL = (People) Below Poverty Line; APL = (People) Below Poverty Line

The rapid and continuously rising PDS Central Issue Prices have resulted in retail Ration-Shop Prices, nullifying the basic objective of providing essential goods to the poor consumers at affordable prices;

but, in spite of this, Food-Subsidies could not be brought down to the desired levels because of continuously rising MSPs. The amount of Food-Subsidy, of the Central Government since 1991-92, is shown in the following table.

Table-5: Food Subsidy of the government of India

YEAR	FOOD SUBSIDY (Rs. crore)
1991-1992	2850
1995-1996	5377
1999-2000	9200
2000-2001	12150
2001-2002	13675

Sources: Economic Survey, 2000-2001, p.96; Statistical Outline of India, Tata Services Ltd

Form the above table, it is seen that Food-Subsidy increased from Rs. 2850 crore in 1991-92 to Rs. 13675 crore (about 5 times) in 2001-2002.

To facilitate implementation of Structural Adjustment Programme in India, the "Fiscal Responsibility and Budget Management Bill, 2000" was introduced in the Indian Parliament in December 2000. According to the Bill, the Central Government shall take appropriate measures to eliminate Revenue Deficit, bring down Fiscal Deficit and build up adequate Revenue Surplus (Economic Survey, 2000-2001, p.49).

Under these circumstances, the objectives of the PDS in India have become quite ambiguous and the government hardly knows how to implement them. Therefore, the future of the PDS in India, particularly its beneficial aspect, has become completely uncertain.

6.3. Comparison with the Arthaśāstra Price Policy

The price policy in Arthaśāstra was basically designed for monarchic rule. So, the question arises if it has any relevance for the democratic India at present.

According to Aiyangar, the following aspects of Arthaśāstra state policies are likely to be relevant for the mixed economy of India today.

i) In the Arthaśāstra state, freedom and regulations were intermixed (Aiyangar, 1949, p.156).

ii) Large scale undertakings were taken over by the state management but scope was left for small enterprises to compete with state enterprises (ibid. p.157).

iii) State factories did not displace private enterprises (ibid. p.157).

iv) Outside the sphere of state monopoly, there was no attempt to restrain the private producers (ibid. p.157)

v) In the interest of the whole community, there were state regulations as regards interest, wages, profits and rent. But the state's position was that private liberty should be the rules except where it had to be restrained and regulated either in the interest of the common people or to maintain stability.

vi) Emphasis was laid on precision, simplification, detail and transparency as regards all state affairs, e.g.

a) All state orders should be in writing.

b) Power and duties of different state departments should be clearly demarcated.

c) Salaries of all public servants should be paid promptly.

d) Accurate data should be available as regards land survey, fiscal collections, types of consumption etc. (ibid. p.165).

Like Aiyangar, we, considering the functioning of the price policy in India in course of fifty years of planning, also think that many features of Arthaśāstra price policy are still relevant for India. In course of our analysis of the Arthaśāstra economy we have seen that in Arthaśāstra, prices were not determined by some whimsical autocrat and imposed on the buyers and sellers from above. Although the superintendent of commerce was entrusted with the task of determining prices, he was to do this on the basis of actual market situations, conditions of demand, supply and cost, prevailing customs etc. A deeper insight makes it clear that he had to fix and enforce those prices which would be automatically determined by the interaction of demand and supply, unhindered by monopolies, vested interests, irregularities and corruption. This is exactly the policy necessary for a less developed democratic country like India.

Notwithstanding the differences in political system, the above mentioned six features of the Arthaśāstra state are not contradictory to the provisions of the democratic Constitution of India today and objectives of planning. If properly adapted and implemented, they are likely to streamline the functioning of various economic policies under planning and remove many hurdles on the path of successful implementation of these policies.

Kauṭilya realized that the traders and artisans, if left alone, would always charge unduly high prices in order to enhance profit and, thereby, generate instability and cause hardships to the common people. To prevent this, direct price control by the state became necessary.

As regards the necessity of price control in India today, L. K. Jha, the ex-governor of the RBI, pointed out (Jha, 1968, pp.478-80) that prices in an LDC like India cannot be left to be determined by market forces where, instead of free competition, monopolistic control prevails. Direct price control becomes necessary in India, according to Jha, for the following reasons:

i) To protect the interests of the vulnerable sections of the population.

ii) To guide investments to the desired channels.

iii) To prevent hoarders from increasing prices by taking advantage of shortages.

Thus we see, that in spite of the differences in political system, the basic objectives of Kauṭilya's price policy resemble the Administered Price Policy under the five year plans in India. But the Arthaśāstra price policy distinguishes itself by the following features:

a) Unlike in India, fiscal and monetary measures were not at all relevant for price policy in the age of Arthaśāstra. Only direct price control measures were relevant.

b) The Arthaśāstra state always refrained from unnecessary control (2.16.)

c) Commodities were to be sold at market places specified by the state (2.21.)

d) Commodities were to be sold only after they were precisely weighed, measured, numbered and marked by government 'seal' (2.21).

e) The price, whatever it is, should be announced by the seller (2.21.)

f) Price increase by haggling was discouraged (2.21.)

g) Prices were rigidly fixed by the state against market forces only if excess demand or supply were temporary. In case of persistent discrepancy, prices were permitted to vary according to demand and supply. But suitable adjustments were made by the state alone. Private producers and merchants were never permitted to do this on their own.

h) Price policy was accompanied by suitable administrative and legal measures for its proper implementation.

The above mentioned features were essential for successful implementation of the price policy of Arthaśāstra. They were devised with a monarchic rule in mind. But a deeper insight would reveal that they are not at all antagonistic to the democratic system. So, these features, if emulated after necessary modifications, are likely to convert the 'Ill-Administered' price policy in India under planning to a 'Well-Administered' one.

6.4. Conclusion

The basic features of the price policy pursued in India during the plan period are"

i) Administered prices of various agricultural commodities.

ii) Vast subsidies arising out of the endeavour to fulfill simultaneously the contradictory objectives of providing price incentives to the producers and provision of low-priced essential goods to the consumers.

The above features, however, have led to many undesirable effects on the Indian economy. The Seventh and Eighth Plans (Planning Commission), various issues of Report on Currency and Finance (RBI) and Economic Survey (Govt. of India) reveal many disquieting features of the Administered Price Policy. In fact, instead of having control over the prices, the price controlling authorities are themselves being controlled by extraneous forces which compel them to raise prices at inappropriate moments leading to many adverse repercussions on the economy. The recent hike in the prices of petroleum products is a glaring example of the helplessness of the price controlling authorities in India. In fact, the price policy during the plan period in India has played the 'boomerang'. Instead of controlling inflation it has aggravated the inflationary situation (V. Pandit, 1993).

So, to make our Administered Price Policy successful, we may emulate the essential features of Arthaśāstra Price Policy. An integral element of Arthaśāstra Price Policy was the administrative and legal set up necessary for its proper implementation.

So, in India today, appropriate administrative and legal set up accompany price policy. We may tone up our administrative and legal set up and emulate many features of Arthaśāstra economy in this regard without violating any provisions of our democratic political set up. One important problem remains as regards the emulation of the Espionage Network, which was an essential ingredient of Arthaśāstra Price Policy.

Notwithstanding the fact that there are evidences of ghastly activities of Espionage Networks of many modern states (Dallin, 1955; Furago, 1961, 1962; Gramont, 1962; West, 1964), Kauṭilya-type exhaustive Espionage Network is not desirable in a democratic country like India. In a limited scale, however, intelligence network is always necessary to maintain administrative efficiency and suppress corruption. Secret agencies like the Central Bureau of Investigations (CBI), Intelligence Branch, Special Branch, Enforcement Department (ED), Vigilance Department, etc. are essential for proper functioning of the government and to fight crime and corruption. Nobody is likely to consider the CBI's actions, against the unscrupulous politicians, undemocratic. Moreover, the vast Espionage Network of Kauṭilya was an alternative to the quick transport and communication facilities, which were lacking in Kauṭilya's time (Bharati Mukherjee, 1976, p.42). Now-a-days, these tasks of Arthaśāstra spies may be easily handled by using computer networks.

So we conclude that emulation of the basic features of Arthaśāstra Price Policy is likely to improve immensely the performance of our price policy under Economic Planning and it may even make our price policy perfectly successful.

In the newly emerging era, integration of the Indian Economy with the global economic system is not possible if there are rigidities, irregularities and lack of transparency, generated by monopolies, vested interests, 'ballot-box' politics etc. in our price policy. The operation of the pricing mechanism within the Indian economy is to be streamlined in conformity with the needs of LPG (Liberalization, Privatization and Globalization) and in this regard, Kauṭilya's methods (constructed by an exquisite mixture of traditional ideas with global influences emanating from Greece, Persia, Syria, and Egypt) may be of much help.

Chapter-7: Verification of Hypothesis

7.1. Introduction

In this chapter, we are going to verify the hypotheses put forward in Chapter-1 [1.6.2], viz.

a) There is a systematic and coherent price control mechanism implied in Arthaśāstra.

b) In contrast to the price control mechanism in Arthaśāstra, the Administered Price Policy pursued in India during the plan period is inconsistent and *ad hoc* in nature.

c) The method (in a modified form), as available in Arthaśāstra, may be utilized to devise a coherent 'Administered Price Policy' in a democratic set up as in India.

Let us now examine, on the basis of the preceding six chapters, how far the above hypotheses are tenable.

7.2. Hypothesis (a): Systematic and Coherent Price Control Mechanism in Arthaśāstra

Principles regarding price determination and maintenance of these prices are scattered in various chapters in Arthaśāstra (in the form of Kauṭilya-style brief but precise statements). In chapter-4 of this study, we have pieced together these statements and brought out the salient features of Arthaśāstra Price Policy, which may be stated briefly in the following manner:

i) Arthaśāstra emphasizes maintenance of a just price, which is to be determined as:

P (Just Price) = Production Cost + Tolls and Taxes + Transport and Associated Costs + Profit.

Production Cost = Raw Material Cost + Wages + Interest.

We have seen in chapter-4 of this study that Arthaśāstra laid down specific principles to determine the above ingredients of 'just price'.

ii) In the Arthaśāstra economy Superintendent of Commerce and Superintendent of Tolls House were entrusted with the task of enforcing these just prices.

iii) Methods of implementation and enforcement of 'just price' were inexorably associated with the price policy enumerated in Arthaśāstra. The implementation network consisted of: Administrative Set Up; Espionage Network; Accounting and Auditing Mechanism and Buffer Stock.

iv) There were specific measures to detect all conceivable types of violation of price control rules by producers, traders and government officials. Violations were subject to punishment according to the degree of offence.

v) Arthaśāstra always gave proper consideration to the market forces of demand and supply while determining and controlling prices. There were no attempts to hold prices at rigid levels against the forces of demand and supply. In case of persistent discrepancy, prices were altered by 'trial-and-error' method to restore balance between demand and supply.

From the above five observations, it is clear that there was no *ad hoc* decisions as regards price determination and maintenance of the determined prices in the Arthaśāstra economy.

We have also seen that the methods of price determination in Arthaśāstra are amenable to mathematical treatment (discussed in detail in Appendix to chapter-5 of this study).

So from the above observations we may come to the conclusion that Arthaśāstra Price Policy was systematic and coherent.

7.3. Hypothesis (b): *Ad hoc* and Inconsistent Nature of 'Administered Price Policy' in India during the Plan Period

The *ad hoc* and incoherent nature of administered price policy in India during the plan period is revealed from the following facts.

i) In chapter-6 of this study, we have discussed in detail that "Administered Price Policy' during the plan period in India was not guided by any uniform and consistent rules. Prices were revised according to the exigencies of extraneous forces, designs of the vested interest groups and political pressure groups, and situations arising out of financial mismanagement. In fact, price revisions were *ad hoc* in nature and there were no basic principles on the basis of which prices were revised.

ii) In theory, administered prices were to be determined by cost-plus rule, but this was not backed up by proper accounting measures and adequate statistical information.

iii) There were no principles on the basis of which commodities, the prices of which are to be administered, were selected.

iv) In many cases, attempts were made to keep prices rigidly fixed against long term supply demand conditions. But, ultimately, the price controlling authorities had to yield and raise prices at inappropriate times (e.g., sudden increases in the prices of petroleum products, cooking gas etc.).

v) Attempts were made to provide consumer goods to weaker sections of population at low prices and at the same time there were also attempts to preserve the interests of the producers. This resulted in vast subsidies. The above policies were pursued without calculating the possible amount of subsidies and considering whether the government would be able to bear the burden of subsidies for an indefinite period of time.

vi) Price policy was not accompanied by appropriate measures to implement it.

vii) 'Administered Price Policy' was devised more by the dictates of the vested interest and political pressure groups, and 'ballot-box' politics than by consideration of economic interests of the country and welfare of the majority of the population.

viii) Instead of having control over prices, the price controlling authorities in India today are themselves being controlled by extraneous forces, which compel them to raise prices at inappropriate times leading to many adverse repercussions on the economy. In fact, sporadic increase in administered prices is one of the major causes of hyperinflation in India in recent years.

Thus we see that 'Administered Price Policy' during the plan period in India has been ill administered and has created more problems than it has solved. This certainly brings to the fore the *ad hoc* and inconsistent aspects of 'Administered Price Policy' during the plan period in India.

7.4. Hypothesis (c): Utility of Arthaśāstra Price Policy to Devise a Coherent Administered Price Policy for a Democratic Country like India

As regards the necessity of continuance of administered prices even after the enunciation of the New Economic Policy based on LPG in 1991, we reiterate the *raison d'être* mentioned by L. K. Jha (discussed in detail in chapter-6 of this study):

i) To protect the interests of the vulnerable sections of the population.

ii) To guide investments in the desired channels.

iii) To prevent hoarders from increasing prices by taking advantage of shortages.

Very few would disagree with the justifiability of the above grounds for introducing administered prices of some mass consumption goods and essential inputs. The administered price policy is being criticized simply because it could fulfill none of the above objectives. On the contrary, it generated some serious problems with long-term adverse consequences for the Indian economy.

In this connection, our hypothesis is that the shortcomings of the administered price policy could be overcome if we emulate the basic principles (with appropriate modifications) of Arthaśāstra price policy.

The pertinent question here is:

If price policy devised for monarchy (Arthaśāstra was basically devised for monarchy) could be emulated in a democratic set up as in India today.

Our answer in this regard is: "Certainly".

To substantiate this assertion, we first put forward the following assumptions:

a) 'Democratic Government' means a welfare-oriented institution instead of a machinery to implement the design of vested interest and political pressure groups.

b) Election considerations do not force the government (which is run by legislators elected from one or a 'a group of' political parties in a democratic set up) to adopt policies contrary to the interest of the nation and that of the common people.

c) Corruption of government officials could be minimized by proper measures of vigilance and punishment.

The basic reasons of failure of the 'Administered Price Policy' in India today are:

i) Policies devised without paying attention to appropriate measures to implement them.

ii) Prices fixed at the behest of the vested interest and political pressure groups.

iii) Pricing based on imperfect accounting method and inadequate statistical information.

iv) Widespread corruption among government officials.

v) Pricing, in many cases, based on vast subsidies, disregarding the long-term consequences.

vi) Lon-term supply-demand conditions not proper attention to.

vii) Inadequate buffer stock to absorb short-term discrepancies.

Of the shortcomings as mentioned above, the second and fourth items are ruled out in an ideal democratic system according to our assumption. As regards the other shortcomings, the Arthaśāstra price policy is likely to provide a way out.

By emulating the Arthaśāstra principles, administered prices could be determined by giving proper consideration to short-run and long-run supply-demand conditions and on the basis of perfect and up-to-date statistical information. Among the implementation measures in Arthaśāstra, "Proper Administrative Setup', 'Perfect Audit and Accounting', and 'Adequate Buffer Stock' could be adopted in India today without violating the basic principles of our democratic constitution.

The only questionable aspect among the Arthaśāstra implementation measures is the vast "Espionage Network", which may not be desirable in a democratic country like India (notwithstanding the fact that modern democracies like the USA, France, U.K. etc. place much reliance on powerful transnational Espionage Networks).

In a limited scale, however, intelligence agencies like the Central Bureau of Investigations (CBI), Enforcement Department (ED), Special Branch (SB), Vigilance Departments (VDs) etc. are necessary for proper functioning of the administrative machinery, defence mechanism, foreign policy, etc., and to suppress crime and corruption in a democratic country like India.

Moreover, we have discussed in chapter-1 [1.3.2] of this study that espionage mechanism was necessary in Kauṭilya's time as an alternative to communication network, which was rudimentary in those days as compared to modern communication systems. In fact, it is not necessary now-a-days, to resort to unethical espionage mechanism for dissemination of information relating to implementation of price policy. This could be easily accomplished, today, with the assistance of a chain of computers interlinked through the 'Internet'. Computers are also capable of handling complications of modern economies with vast number of commodities and complicated interrelations among them.

In chapter-5 of this study, we have arranged the Arthaśāstra prices in an input-output model, which could be extended (without violating the Arthaśāstra principles) for a modern economy with a very large number of commodities and complicated input-output relationships. Now-a-days, with the help of appropriate soft wares, an ordinary clerk can easily handle these complicated models.

7.4.2. Modifications for Monetary and Fiscal Policies

We have seen in chapter-2 of this study that rapid inflationary rise in money supply was not possible in Arthaśāstra setup. Rapid bank credit expansion, too, was not possible in those days. Moreover, fiscal and budgetary deficits were not permissible in Arthaśāstra principles. So, monetary and fiscal factors did not affect the price policy in Arthaśāstra state. But today, over-supply of money and budgetary deficits are two important factors affecting prices. So price policy now-a-days must attach much importance to monetary and fiscal measures for price control. Kauṭilya's method may be suitably modified in conformity with these factors, i.e. price policy in India today should be integrated with suitable monetary and fiscal policies.

Thus we see that Kauṭilya's method (in a modified form), as available in Arthaśāstra may be utilized to devise a coherent 'Administered Price Policy' in a democratic setup as in India at present.

7.5. Conclusion

The basic objective of this study was to spell out the salient features of Kauṭilya's price policy as scattered in various chapters of Arthaśāstra and to bring to the fore their relevance for the Indian economy since independence.

We have posed these basic issues in the form of three major hypotheses and have tested their validity in the light of discussions in the preceding six chapters. Although the method of verification, because of the nature of the problem, could not be in the form of conventional statistical hypothesis test (it has been done instead with deductive and inductive reasoning), we may conclude that from our above analysis that the methods of price control as, delineated in Arthaśāstra, are of much relevance for India during the plan period. Moreover, Kauṭilya's period was characterized by global influences from Persia, Syria, Egypt and specifically, Seleucid Greece. In that period every aspect of Indian life (art, literature, coinage, economic and political administration, philosophy, mathematics, science etc.), reveal a fine assimilation of traditional Indian aspects and global influences. So, it was a period of India's encounter with globalization (although at a limited scale) and Kauṭilya's Arthaśāstra may be considered as an important guideline in the era of globalization (in the ancient form). So, in the modern era of globalization, it is likely to provide essential guidelines for successful implementation of the NEP and integration of the Indian economy with the world economy without causing damage to our national features.

SELECT BIBLIOGRAPHY

Aiyangar, K.V. Rangaswami (1934): *Aspects of Ancient Indian Economic Thought*, B. H. U., Banaras.

Aiyangar, K.V. Rangaswami (1949): *Indian Cameralism, a Survey of Some Aspects of Arthasastra*, the Adyar Library, Madras, India.

Altekar, A. S. (1962): *State and Government in Ancient India*, Motilal Banarasidass, Delhi.

Anjaria, J. J. (1935): The Nature and Grounds of Political Obligations in Hindu State, Longman, Green & Co.

Bagchi, U. N. (1926): The Law og Minerals in Ancient India, Calcutta.

Ballantyne, James R. (translator) (1885): Sankhya Aphorisms of Kapila, Trubner & Co., Ludgate Hill, London.

Bandopadhyay, N. C. (1927): Development of Hindu Polity and Political Theories, Calcutta.

————————————————(1925): Economic Life and Progress in Ancient India, C. U.

.... (1927): Kautilya, An Exposition of His Social Ideal and Political Theory, Calcutta.

Banerjee, P. N. (1916): Public Administration in Ancient India, Macmillan & Co.

Barnett, L. D. (1977): Antiquities of India, Punthi Pustak, Calcutta.

Basham, A. I. (1954): The Wonder That Was India, Sidwick and Jackson, London.

Basu, Ratan Lal (1999): "Material Progress and Ethics: a Pilgrimage Through Time", in The Culture Mandala (The Bulletin of the Center for East-West Cultural and Economic Studies, Bond University, Australia), Vol.4, No.1, December 1999-January 2000 (http://www.international-relations.com).

Basu, Ratan Lal (2005) "Why the Human Development Index Does not Measure up to Ancient Indian Standards" in The Culture Mandala (The Bulletin of the Center for East-West Cultural and Economic Studies, Bond University, Australia), Vol.6, No.2, January 2005. [http://www.international-relations.com].

Basu, Ratan Lal (2005): "Human Development Part 2: Ancient Kingship, Modern Politicians and the Problem of Corruption in India" in The Culture Mandala, Vol.7, No.1, December 2005.

Beniprasad (1928): The State in Ancient India, Allahabad.

Bhandarkar, D. R. (1929): Some Aspects of Ancient Hindu Polity, B. H. U., Banaras.

Bhargava, P. L. (1935): Chandragupta Maurya, Lucknow.

Blackstock, Paul, W. (1964): The Strategy of Subversion, Manipulating the Policies of Other Nations, Quadrangle Books, Chicago.

Bose, Atindranath (1945): (Vols. 1 & 2): Social and Rural Economy of Northern India, C. U.

Brahmananda, P. R. (1980): Growthless Inflation with Stockless Money, Himalaya Publishing Co., Bombay.

Broloer, B. (1929-34): Kautilya Studies (3 vols): Bonn.

Buch, M.A. (1979): *Economic Life in Ancient India*, R.S. Publishing House, Allahabad.

Chakladar, H. C. (1929): Social Life in Ancient India, Calcutta.

Chaudhuri, R. K. (1971): Kautilya's Political Ideas and Institutions, Chaukhamba Publication, Varanasi.

Chinnock, E. J. (English translation, 1893): Arrian's "Anabasis of Alexander and India", London.

Chunder, Pratap Chandra (1970): Kautilya on Love and Morals, Calcutta.

Chunder, Pratap Chandra (1995): *Kautilya's Arthasastra*, The M. P. Birla Foundations, Calcutta.

Clark, Christopher (2007): *Iron Kingdom: The Rise and Downfall of Prussia, 1600-1947*, Penguin, New York.

Cosmas: *Christian Topography* (http://www.scribd.com/doc/131184581/Cambridge-Library-Collection-Hakluyt-First-Series-Cosmas-Indicopleustes-Edited-and-Translated-By-J-W-McCrindle-The-Christian-Topography-of-Cos)

Dallin, David J. (1955): *Soviet Espionage*, Yale University Press, New Haven.

Dantzig, G. B. (1963): Linear Programming and Extensions, Princeton University Press, New Jersey.

Das, S. K. (1925): Economic Life in Ancient India, Calcutta.

Dasgupta, S. N. & Dey, S. K. (eds.) (1962): *A History of Sanskrit Literature, Vol. I*, University of Calcutta.

Dikshitar, V. R. R. (1932): The Mauryan Polity, Madras University.

Dorfman, Samuelson and Solow (1958): Linear Programming and Economic Analysis, McGraw-Hill Book Co. Inc., New York.

Dutt, Benode Behari (1925): Town Planning in Ancient India, Calcutta.

Dutt, Ruddar (2001): "Economic Lliberalisation and its Implications for Employment in India" in *the Conference Volume*, 84th Annual Conference of the Indian Economic Association, Vellore, Tamil Nadu.

Engels, Frederic (1884): *The Origin of the Family, Private Property and the State*, Moscow, Progress Publishers, Eighth Printing, 1972.

Furago, Ladislas (1961): Burn after Reading, the Espiuonage History of World War II, Walker, New York.

Furago, Ladislas (1962): *War and Wits*, Paperback Library, New York.

Gadgil, D.R. (1973): Industrial Evolution in India in Recent Times, 1860-1939; Oxford University Press, Delhi.

Geetha, S. & Suryanarayana, M. H. (1993): "Revamping PDS: Some Issues and Implications" EPW, Vol. XXVIII, No. 41, October 9.

Ghosal, U. N. (1929): Contribution to the History of the Hindu Revenue System, Calcutta.

Ghosal, U. N. (1957): Studies in Indian History and Culture, Orient Longman, Bombay.

Ghosal, U. N. (1959): A History of Indian Political Ideas, Oxford University Press, Bombay.

Gopal, M. H. (1935): Mauryan Public Finance, London.

Government of India: Economic Survey, various issues.

Gowen, H. N. (1929): "The Indian Machiavelli", Pol. Sc. Quarterly, vol. 44, pp. 173-92.

Gramont, S. D. (1962): The Secret War, Putnam, New York.

Hamilton and Falconer (1854-57): Strabo's Geography (3 vols.), London.

Hindu, The (1966): Survey of Indian Industry.

Hopkins, E. W. (1889): "The Social and Military Position of the Ruling Caste in Ancient India", Journal of American Oriental Society.

Intriligator, Michael D. (1980): Econometric Models, Prentice Hall of India Private Ltd., New Delhi.

Jayaswal, K. P. (1967): *Hindu Polity*, Bangalore Printing and Publishing Co. Ltd., Bangalore City, India.

Jha, L. K. (1968): "Price Policy in Developing Economy", RBI Bulletin, April 20.

Jolly, J. (1923): Arthasastra of Kautilya, Motilal Banarasi Dass, Lahore.

Kane, P. V. (1930): History of Dharmasastras, Bhandarkar Oriental Research Institute, Poona.

Kangle, R. P. (2010): *Kautiliya Arthasastra* (English translation), 7th Reprint, Motilal Banarasidass Publishers Private Limited, Delhi.

Kann, Robert A. (1974): *A History of the Habsburg Empire: 1526-1918*, California Press.

Kant, Immanuel (1795): "Perpetual Peace", in his *Principles of Politics*, trans. W. Hastie, Clark, Edinburgh, 1891.

Keith, A. B. (1956): Classical Sanskrit Literature, Y. M. C. A. Publishing House, Calcutta.

Konow, Sten (1945): Kautilya Studies, Oslo.

Kosambi, D. D. (1956): An Introduction to the Study of Indian History, Popular Book Depot, Bombay.

.... (1981): The Culture and Civilization of Ancient India, Vikas Publishing House, New Delhi.

Laertius, Diogenes (2001) (tr. R. D. Hicks): *Lives of Eminent Philosophers, Vol. I*, Harvard University Press.

Law, N. N. (1914): Studies in Ancient Hindu Polity Based on Arthasastra of Kautilya, Longman, Green & Co., New York.

.... (1921): Aspects of Ancient Indian Polity, Oxford.

Machiavelli: *The Prince*, (translated by W. K. Marriot) (http://www.gutenberg.org/files/1232/1232-h/1232-h.htm)

Mahajan, V. D. (1983): Ancient India, S. ChaND & Co. Ltd., New Delhi.

Majumdar, R. C. (1960): *Ancient India*, Motilal Banarasidass, Delhi.

.... (1969): Corporate Life in Ancient India, Firma K. L. Mukhopadhyay, Calcutta.

.... (1980): The History and Culture of Indian People, vol. II, Bharatiya Vidya Bhawan, Bombay.

Marx & Engels (1848): *Manifesto of the Communist Party*, Progress Publishers, Moscow 1975.

Max Müller, F. (ed.): *Sacred Books of the East, Vol. XXV*, Oxford Clarendon Press, 1886.

McCrindle, J. W. (1896): *The Invasion of India by Alexander the Great as Described by O. Curtias, Diodorus, Plutarch and Justin*, Archibald Constable, West Minster.

McCrindle, J. W. (1901): *Ancient India as Described by classical Literature*, Archibald Constable, West Minster.

.... (1977): Ancient India as described by Megasthenes and Arrian, Calcutta.

Megasthenes: *Indika* [http://www.sdstate.edu/projectsouthasia/upload/Megasthene-Indika.pdf

Meyer, J. J. (1927): Arthasastra of Kautilya, Leipzig, Otto Harrassowitz.

Mokerjee, R. K. (1920): Local Self Government of Ancient India, Oxford.

Mookerji, R.K. (1980): "Economic Conditions" in Majumdar, R.C. (ed.), *The History and Culture of Indian People, Vol.-II*, Bharatiya Vidya Bhawan, Bombay.

Mukherjee, Bharati (1976): *Kautilya's Concept of Diplomacy*, Minerva Associates, Pvt., Ltd., Calcutta.

Nag, A. K. & Samanta, G. P. (1994): "Inflation in India during the 80's", EPW, Vol. XXIX, No.8, February 19.

Panchamukhi, V. R. (2000): *Indian Classical Thoughts on Economic Development and Management*, Bookwell Publishers, New Delhi.

Pandit, V. (1993): "Controlling Inflation, Some Analytical and Empirical Issues", EPW, Vol. XXVIII, Nos. 1 & 2, January 2-9.

Panikkar, K.M. (1938): The Origin and Evolution of Kingship in Ancient India, Baroda.

Panikkar, K.M. (1966): *A Survey of Indian History*, Asia Publishing House, Bombay.

Pergitar, F. E. (1922): Ancient IndianHistorical Tradition, London.

Periplus: *The Periplus of the Erythraean Sea* [http://www.fordham.edu/halsall/ancient/periplus.asp.]

Planning Commission: 7th and 8th Five Year Plans.

Plato: *Laws* (http://plurality-press.info/wp-content/uploads/2011/07/Laws-by-Plato.pdf)

Plato (1901): *The Republic*, edited and translated by Benjamin Jowett, P. F. Collier & Son, New York.

Pratapgiri, R. (1935): Problem of Indian Polity, Bombay.

Rao, M. V. K. (1953): Studies in Kautilya, Kautiliya Mandali Publication, Mysore.

Rao, M. V. K. (1993): "The Wheat Story, Recent Changes in Price Policy", EPW, Vol. XXVIII, No. 44, October 30.

Rapson, E. J. (1916): Ancient Idia, Cambridge.

Ray, S. R. (1956): Visakha Datta's 'Mudra Rakshasam' (with Eng. Tr.): K. Roy Publisher, Calcutta.

Ray Chowdhury, H. C. (1972): Political History of Ancient India, University of Calcutta.

RBI: Report on Currency and Finance, various issues.

Rhys Davis, C. A. F. (1901): "Economic Conditions in Ancient India", Economic Journal, September.

Samaddar, J. N. (1912): The Glories of Magadha, Calcutta.

.... (1922): Lectures on Economic Conditions of Ancient India, Calcutta.

Santra, Prof. S.C. (ed.) (2001): *Current Perspective of Environmental Science*, Department of Environmental Science, University of Kalyani, Nadia, West Bengal.

Sarkar, Benoy Kumar (1914): Positive Background of Hindu Sociology, Panini Office, Allahabad.

.... (1922): The Political Institutions and the Theories of the Hindus, Verlag Ven Market, Leipzig.

Śāstri, K. A. Nilakanta (ed.) (1967): Age of the Nandas and Mauryas, Motilal Banarasidass, Delhi.

Śāstri, T. Ganapati (edited) (1924): *The Arthasastra of Kautilya, Volume III*, Trivandrum Sanskrit Series, N0. LXXXII.
(https://ia801602.us.archive.org/20/items/ Trivandrum_Sanskrit_Series_TSS/ TSS-082_Arthasastra_Of_Kautilya_with_Tika_Part_3_-_TG_Śāstri_1925.p

Sen, Ajit Kumar (1926): Studies in Hindu Political Thought, L. M. Gupta, Calcutta.

Sen, Amartya (1987): *On Ethics and Economics*, Oxford University Press, New Delhi, Third Impression, 1999.

Sen, Benoy Chandra (1967): Economics in Kautilya, Sanskrit College, Calcutta.

Sen, Satyendra Nath (1976): *Manusmṛti, Chapter-VII* (English translation),Vidyodaya Series No.16, Chattopadhyaya Brothers, Calcutta.

Shamaśāstry, Dr. R. (1923): *Kautilya Arthasastram*, Mysore Printing and Publishing House, Mysore.

Shamaśāstry, R (1967): *Kautilya's Arthasastra*, (Eng. Tr.): Mysore Printing and Publishing House, Mysore.

Shamaśāstry, R (1967): Evolution of Indian Polity, Mysore.

Sharma, Ram Sharan (1959): Aspects of Political Ideas and Institutions in Ancient India, Motilal Banarasidass, Delhi.

Sharma, Sri Ram (1956): Ancient Indian History and Culture, Hind Kitabs Ltd., Bombay.

Shirokov, G. K. (1980): Industrialisation of India; People's Publishing House, New Delhi.

Simpson, Peter L. P. (1997): *The Politics of Aristotle: Translation, Analysis, and Notes*, University of North Carolina Press, Chapel Hill.

Sinha, H. N. (1938): Sovereignty in Ancient Indian Polity, London.

Smith, V. A. (1958): Early History of India, Oxford, Clarendon Press.

Southgate, G. W. (1965): English Economic History; J. M. Dent & Sons Ltd.

Spellman, J. W. (1958): Political Theory of Ancient India, Oxford.

Stein, O. (1921): Megasthenes Und Kautilya, Wien.

Strabo: *Geography* (http://penelope.uchicago.edu/Thayer/E/Roman/Texts/Strabo/home.html).

Strauss, Leo: *Thoughts on Machiavelli* (http://www.amazon.com/gp/reader/
0226777022?v=search-inside&keywords=teacher+of+evil).

Subba Rao, N. S. (1911): Economic and Political Conditions in Ancient India, Mysore.

Thapar, Romila (1990): *A History of India, Volume 1*, Penguin Books, New Delhi and London. Tripathi, R. (1981): History of Ancient India, Motilal Banarasi Dass, Delhi.

Tripathy, R. (1981): History of Ancient India, Motilal Banarasidass, Delhi.

Varma, P. P. (1954): Studies in Hindu Political Thought and its Metaphysical Foundations, Motilal Banarasidass, Delhi.

West, Rebecea (1964): The New Meaning of Treason, Viking, New York.

Winternitz (1959): A history of Sanskrit Literature (tr. S. Ketkar), C. U.